INSPIRATIONS
OF A
NATION

INSPIRATIONS OF A NATION

Tribute to 25 Singaporean South Asians

Edited by
Abhijit Nag

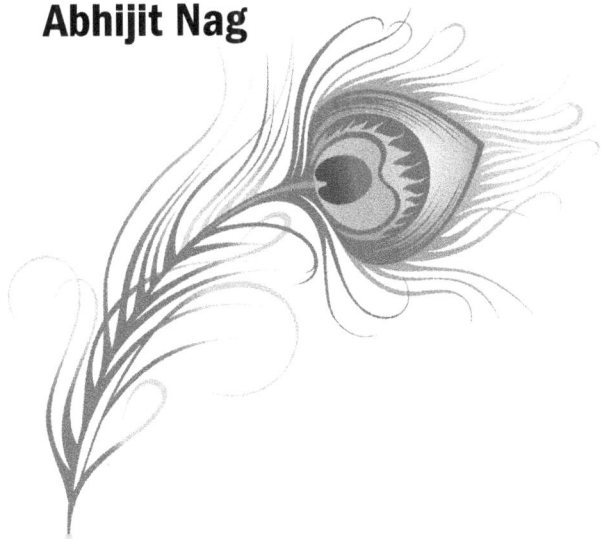

Published by

World Scientific Publishing Co. Pte. Ltd.

5 Toh Tuck Link, Singapore 596224

USA office: 27 Warren Street, Suite 401-402, Hackensack, NJ 07601

UK office: 57 Shelton Street, Covent Garden, London WC2H 9HE

National Library Board, Singapore Cataloguing in Publication Data
Names: Nag, Abhijit, editor.
Title: Inspirations of a nation : tribute to 25 Singaporean South Asians / edited by Abhijit Nag.
Description: Singapore : World Scientific Publishing Co Pte Ltd, [2016]
Identifiers: OCN 940929467 | ISBN 978-981-3141-05-6 (paperback) |
   ISBN 978-981-3141-04-9 (hardback)
Subjects: LCSH: East Indians--Singapore--History. | East Indians--Singapore--Anecdotes. |
   Pioneers--Singapore. | Nationalism and collective memory--Singapore.
Classification: LCC DS610.25.E37 | DDC 305.8914105957--dc2

The views of the Publisher, Writers and Contributors do not reflect the views of the Singapore Memory Project (SMP), which is a national initiative of the Ministry of Communications and Information (MCI) and is managed by the National Library Board, Singapore (NLB).

Whilst reasonable care has been undertaken to ensure the accuracy of the information in this publication, the Publisher, MCI and the NLB accept no legal liabilities whatsoever for the contents of this publication.

Desk Editor: Sandhya Venkatesh
Designer: Jimmy Low

CONTENTS

CONTENTS

PREFACE

Singapore may be only a speck on the world map, but it is a port of call which has had people coming and going for ages. For many, it has been a magnet where they got stuck forever and made a new life for themselves and their families. The first census, in January 1824, recorded 10,683 residents, comprising 74 Europeans, 16 Armenians, 15 Arabs, 4,580 Malays, 3,317 Chinese, 756 natives of India and 1,925 Bugis. Now the population has grown to 5.47 million. Indians, however, remain a small minority, making up just 9.1 per cent of the 3.8-million resident populations. Nevertheless, Indians have played a notable role in the development of Singapore.

They came with Stamford Raffles. When he arrived in Singapore in January 1819, he brought with him about 120 sepoys and lascars, assistants and servants. Also with him came Narayana Pillay, an Indian trader from Penang, who built the Sri Mariamman Temple, Singapore's oldest Hindu temple, in 1827.

Indians helped build and defend the British settlement. Indian sepoys garrisoned Singapore. Indian convicts, sent here till the 1860s, helped build roads, public works and buildings, including the beautiful St Andrew's Cathedral. Indians joined the police force, worked for the government, entered various trades and professions and made their mark as teachers, doctors and lawyers.

Here are some of their stories. Meet Albel Singh, the first Singaporean to register for national service; Kripa Ram Vij, the first army chief; and Bala Subramanion, the first postmaster general.

Do you remember Dr BR Sreenivasan? He was the first vice chancellor of the University of Singapore, which later became the National University of Singapore. We also recall the lives and achievements of Velauthur Ambiavagar, the first Asian headmaster of Raffles Institution, Dr James MJ Supramaniam, the pioneer TB doctor, the broadcasters S Chandramohan and Ananda Perera, and the Vietnam War photographer Chellappah Canagaratnam.

Read the love story of George Suppiah, the first Asian to be a World Cup referee. Colourful, too, was the life of union leader G Kandasamy, who led the 1952 postal workers' strike. That was the strike that helped Lee Kuan Yew become a leader; he himself mentioned that in his memoirs.

Did you know that Eugene Wijeysingha, the renowned former headmaster of Raffles Institution, became a teacher just so he could go to university? We also hear the life story of Professor Edwin Thumboo, the eminent poet and academic, who had an Indian father and a Chinese mother. The acclaimed musician Alex Abisheganaden regaled us with his memories of yesteryear, which included singing Japanese songs on the radio and meeting the Queen in Buckingham Palace.

It's remarkable, the anecdotes that surfaced. Wildlife consultant Subaraj Rajathurai, for example, reminisced about the day he gave Prime Minister Lee Hsien Loong a snake to wear around his neck for a photo op at Pulau Ubin in 2014.

Sportsmen and athletes naturally had some of the most memorable stories. Malaccan-born PC Suppiah recalled running for Singapore to become a Singapore citizen. No less remarkable is the life story of the former sprint queen Glory Barnabas, still competing and winning medals past the age of 70. Singapore's sole boxing Olympian Syed Abdul Kadir is busy as ever, running his own boxing school. Former sprinter UK Shyam, who became Singapore's fastest man when he ran 100 metres in 10.37 seconds in 2001, is a lecturer now teaching philosophy and political science at Hwa Chong Institution.

It was a pleasure working on this book because some of the people we met — high-flyers who are, nevertheless, modest and down-to-earth. They saw nothing unusual about themselves and wondered why we are writing about them. The answers will emerge in the following pages, we hope, replete with their stories and achievements.

As Singapore celebrates 50 years of independence, it's something to cherish — this sense of nationhood that transcends race, religion and culture. To recall a popular National Day song, we are One People, One Nation, One Singapore.

ACKNOWLEDGEMENT

First and foremost, I would like to express my gratitude to President SR Nathan for his interest and advice on the publication, and Abhijit Nag, to whom I shall remain indebted. My gratitude is also due to Balji PN, Gim Lee, Johnson Davasagayam, Ng Loke Koon, Samuel S. Dhoraisingam, my advisors for this publication. I would also like to thank the art director Jee Cheng, for her patience and diligence, as well as Ambika Raghavan, Ashwin Umapathi, Singapore Polytechnic Senior Lecturer M Thiyagarajan and Director, V Maheantharan and students, Clifford Kee Weng Siong, Florence Tan, Muhammad Raihan bin Ripin, Nur Hiddayh bte Abdullah for all their assistance throughout this project.

It has been a joy to learn of the extraordinary stories of all 25 featured personalities and I would like to thank them for their time and warm hospitality in welcoming Abhijit and me to their homes.

Last but not least, my gratitude goes to Wan Wee Pin, Yee Yeong Chong, Ler Ka Leng, Lee Ying Ying and Michelle Heng from the National Library Board for their support and grant for this book, without which it would not have been published.

This book is based on an idea by Alfred Dass.

BY ABHIJIT NAG

THE SOUND OF MUSIC

Life is still a lovely tune for Cultural Medallion winner Alex Abisheganaden, who continues to play and teach the guitar when he is not walking the dog or resting at home like any other octogenarian.

The morning showed the day in the life of Alex Abisheganden. The boy who woke up to the sound of music played by his father continues to make music in his late eighties. His gnarled textured old fingers no longer touch the double bass that brought him fame. The classical guitar, however, continues to respond faithfully to his expert touch. Alex remains inseparable from his music as he continues to play and teach the young, who are picking up the chords just the way he did years ago, when the Union Jack still fluttered from government buildings and Singapore was part of the empire on which the sun never set.

It was in the service of the empire that his parents made their home in Singapore, where he came into his own as a musician and received official honours. He was awarded the Cultural Medallion in 1988, two years after his eldest brother, Paul, who was also a musician. However, there are no airs about him. Looking at him, you wouldn't know the unassuming old man was invited to Buckingham Palace, spoke to Queen Elizabeth and played a prominent role in Singapore's cultural landscape.

He has to be coaxed to speak about himself. "You want to interview me?" he asked with a smile. "Thank you," he said, opening the door to his HDB flat in the corner of a high floor from which the trees and constructions below looked like miniature toys. In a batik shirt and trousers, he was a picture of graciousness as he shooed away a pet dog and led the way to the narrow dining room and pulled up a chair. His wife was not at home, the dog was out of earshot, and the room was bathed in afternoon light as he began to talk about the old days.

His parents came from India. They arrived in Penang in the early 1900s. His father, Abisheganathan, had learnt Pitman's shorthand and typewriting in India and was reputed to be a very fast stenographer. From Penang, the couple moved to Singapore, where

Abisheganathan worked in the office of the Colonial Secretary. Alex was born in Singapore on January 31, 1926. He had four brothers and two sisters. The family lived in government quarters in Buffalo Road. Alex recalls his father wearing a white coat and trousers. He always carried a Bible in his pocket. A staunch Christian, he was actively involved in the Tamil Methodist Church and Ceylon Pentecostal Missionary. He played the violin but sang only Tamil songs and hymns. He and his wife woke up early in the morning to read the Bible and sing hymns. They held a prayer meeting every month.

All the boys went to St Andrew's. The school was then located opposite Malaya Publishing House near Stamford Road, where the old Christ Church was. St Joseph's Institution and Raffles Girls' School were also nearby. Both those buildings are still standing today. Alex initially attended a kindergarten, where he learned English. His father would drop him off at Dhoby Ghaut. He was taught by a Tamil lady teacher. So, when he entered St Andrew's, he skipped Primary 1 and 2 and instead went straight to Standard 1.

As a boy, Alex was not into games, but wanted to be a budding musician like his brothers. Paul picked up the violin from his father. Geoffrey was a singer. Gerard played the piano and the cello, and Felix the harmonica. Alex took over Gerard's guitar. "Nobody taught me to play the guitar," he said. He learned how to play from the book, *Ellis through School for the Guitar*.

He was still in school when war broke out. During the Japanese Occupation, he played the guitar in an Indian orchestra for the Azad Hind radio station, which broadcast anti-British propaganda in support of the Indian National Army. He was not anti-British but accepted the job as a musician, playing music at night at the radio station, which was located at Cathay Building. He also learned Japanese and was asked to sing Japanese songs on the radio. After the war, he passed the Senior Cambridge examination and became a teacher. He followed the advice of his eldest brother, Paul, a Raffles College graduate who later served as principal of Victoria School and the Teachers' Training College and taught music at the National University of Singapore for many years.

Alex enjoyed teaching. He attended the Teachers' Training College and was subsequently posted to a school close to Bidadari in Sennett Estate. He continued to play music and became a member of the Singapore Junior Symphony Orchestra. Later, he joined the Singapore Chamber Ensemble founded by his brother, Paul. He played the double bass. He is still grateful for the lessons he had from the Hungarian cellist Feri Krempl. In 1960, Alex became the first person in Southeast Asia to receive a Licentiate of the Royal Schools of Music (LRSM) for performance on the double bass. "I became well-known as a good double bass player," he said with a smile. He also attained Grade Eight for both guitar and voice, clearing the way for higher studies in music.

As teachers could take sabbaticals to study abroad if the course they were interested in was relevant to their work. Alex, on advice by an education official, could apply to study music abroad. Alex left behind his wife, who encouraged him to follow his heart and went to London's Royal College of Music. He studied voice, bass and the guitar in London. His guitar teacher was the famous classical guitarist John Williams.

It was during his student days in London that he met the Queen, He laughed as he recalled the event. One day, a fellow student at the hostel told him, "A police officer wants to see you." Nervously, he went to meet the officer, who turned out to be a representative from Buckingham Palace with an invitation to meet the Queen. The taxi driver could not believe him when, on the appointed day, he hailed a cab and said he wanted to go to the palace. The cabby looked at him and asked if he were drunk!

At the palace, he saw that representatives from every British colony were invited to meet the Queen to celebrate Empire Day. The protocol officer, who briefed them, said they were not to ask the Queen any questions. When Alex met the Queen, she asked if he was enjoying his stay in London. "Yes, this is the best place to learn music," he said. It was a wonderful experience, he recalled, seeing the beautiful palace gardens and meeting people from all over the world.

He resumed teaching after he returned from London. In his early 40s, he became the principal of Cedar Boys' Primary School. Later on he was promoted to inspector of schools.

Alex was also commissioned to produce 26 episodes of the programme *Music Making with the Guitar*, which was broadcast on Education Television (ETV) in 1970 and 1971. He also wrote the two textbooks that accompanied the series. He was a songwriter as well, composing songs for government campaigns. In 1981, he founded the NUS Guitar Ensemble (GENUS), the region's first Niibori guitar ensemble, finishing fourth in an international competition in Germany in 2014.

Alex played his part in theatre, too. He was a founder member of Theatreworks and appeared in operas staged by the National University of Singapore Society.

Alex's mission is to spread beauty in the world through the element of music.

He still has a powerful voice, which boomed when he launched dramatically into the "Atomic Talking Blues." He thumped the table vigorously, keeping a regular beat, as he declaimed sang the lines from the protest song:

"Here's my moral, plain as day,
Old Man Atom is here to stay.
He's gonna hang around, it's plain to see,
But, ah, my dearly beloved, are we?...
Hiroshima, Nagasaki -- here's my text
Hiroshima, Nagasaki -- Lordy, who'll be next."

He talked and sang through the protest song when asked about the other kinds of music he had performed besides Western classical. There is a YouTube video which shows him strumming the guitar and singing the song, but he hasn't seen it. He doesn't even have an email address or a mobile phone. The old fixed phone is good enough for him — that and the guitar, of course. He still teaches the guitar at a music school run by one of his former students.

He shares his talent with his daughter. Jacintha Abisheganaden is an acclaimed singer in her own right. Her HDB flat is right opposite his. His son, Peter Jerome Abisheganaden, has earned his spurs in a different field, as an equestrian. He was a member of the Singapore polo team that took the silver at the 2007 SEA Games.

A smile played on Alex's face when Chestnut walked into the room. The black dog, which belongs to Jacintha, sidled up to him. Alex interpreted Chestnut as saying. "It's time to take Chestnut for a walk," he said. Chestnut wagged its tail happily. The words were music to its ears.

BY VEENA BHARWANI

THE FIRST NSMAN

The first Singaporean to register for national service, Lt-Col Albel Singh (ret) recalls the early days of his three decades in the army.

It was just an ordinary day on 28 March 1967, but it was anything but ordinary for Albel Singh. He was the first Singaporean to register for national service at the Central Manpower Base at Kallang Road among the 900 enlistees at that point. It was a surreal experience to be picked up from a community centre and transported by a military truck to the base at Kallang.

After being the first man in line to register for national service, he had to wait for four months to be called up for basic military training.

He bonded with the institution and profession, and stayed in the Singapore Armed Forces for 32 years. He retired in 1999 as a lieutenant-colonel, commander of the 29th Singapore Infantry Brigade.

As an 18-year-old who had just graduated from secondary school, he was naturally apprehensive when he was called up for national service. He had grown up hearing all sorts of stories about life in the army from his uncles.

On the day he had to go in, there were tearful scenes. He reported to the Cheng San Community Centre and was put on a three-ton truck and taken to the Central Manpower Base.

"As we were leaving, I could see some parents and siblings crying. I cannot recall how many of us were in the truck but it was not crowded. My guess would be that that there were no more than 15 or 16 persons. In the three-ton truck, the mood was sombre. For a long while, there was pin-drop silence. Then someone spoke in dialect. A few others joined in."

At the Central Manpower Base, his identity card was collected before he and the rest were ushered into a big room for the oath-taking led by an army officer by the name of

Ishvarlall Singh. After which, he recalled, they were taken to camp at Taman Jurong. He was issued a plate, a mug, a tray and a fork and spoon. "We were then marched off to the cook house for our very first meal in camp."

Mr Singh, 65, recalled the first thing that recruits had to do was to go for a haircut. He recalled that the point of the haircut was to diminish individuality and chisel everyone into a team player. No self — just a uniformed look. He remembered spending hours ironing every crease on his uniform, which was heavily soaked in starch, and shining his boots till they mirrored his image. He reasoned, "When you see someone smartly dressed, it immediately inspires confidence and builds trust. Being a young and fledgling army, it was vital for us to win the trust of the people. Their trust inspired and motivated us".

The food the recruits ate was a far cry from the cuisine available in the army today. "I opted for the non-Muslim meal. I distinctly remember that the meal consisted of rice (very lumpy), a vegetable (it was a green leafy vegetable, I could not make it out), soup (it was like salt water with oil in it) and a meat (chicken which was so difficult to break with the fork and spoon). Being hungry, I swallowed a couple of spoonfuls with the vegetable and the soup. After the first meal, I requested and was given permission to have Muslim meal. The meat, rice and vegetable were the same, the only difference was that there was curry or *sambal.*"

He and his batchmates were the first to experience the rigours and terrors of army life. One particular incident occurred when he was serving as a combat engineer at Gilman Barracks. It involved a roommate who used to cover himself with a jacket and nervously complained of an eerie feeling that someone seemed to be choking him. Singh told him to remove the jacket and the complaints stopped.

Cut off from family and friends, life could get lonely. When he was a cadet at Pasir Laba, during the weekends, the loneliness was especially palpable. Some, because of this fear and loneliness, skipped training, but he recalled that people back then were rather straight and did not abuse the system.

Ironically, the best place to get rest was the graveyard, which was peaceful and quiet. However,

Lt.Col (ret.) Albel Singh believes, 'You can take the man out of the soldier, but not the soldier out of him".

respect was always a priority for the departed resting there. "We were told to apologise first for intruding and offer prayers. We followed this practice as people feel secure when customs are followed," he said.

As a soldier, he learned the importance of team spirit. You need to have confidence in each other and the soldiers trained for this over the years.

He illustrated the importance of teamwork through an anecdote about running. "It doesn't matter if you are the first one to finish. You keep on running on the spot (*hentak kaki*) until the last man finishes. The same went for obstacle courses — you help each other so that the team finishes faster. Even the Fire and Movement team demonstrates the extreme importance of team work. Some soldiers have to move while others open fire. If there is non-compliance, someone can be killed. If there is a straggler, you cannot fight the enemy."

It was not only training that kept him busy back then; there were serious incidents, too. He remembered the Konfrontasi (Confrontation), which led to two terrorists being hanged in 1968. Singh, only 19, was a corporal in 3 SIR (3rd Singapore Infantry Regiment) at Bedok Camp. Armed with live ammunition, he and his mates were driven to Changi, where they dug and hid in trenches. As a teen, he was terrified to see the Indonesian armada at sea. The vessels were armed with long-range guns, capable of hitting the trenches, but senior officers rallied the young national servicemen, helping them overcome their fears.

Another incident etched in his mind occurred on May 13, 1969, when he was an officer cadet and a platoon commander. He was rudely awakened by the banging on his barrack doors in the early morning, which made him think they had overslept.

They were ordered to fall in and move to Queenstown. On the night they had to patrol Lorong Tai Seng, there were ugly rumours of racial conflict. They had orders to stop people from gathering and spreading false rumours.

From the next day, they were deployed to Paya Lebar police station. "We reached the police station before dark and returned to our camp after first light. This was the routine for more than a week. We slept during the day and patrolled the streets during the night. We patrolled in Land Rovers. Each Land Rover was commanded by an officer and there were two to three cadets and a policeman with him. The team I was in was with our platoon commander. We would go wherever there was any suspicion of trouble. So we spent most of our time patrolling the Lorong Tai Seng area. In those days, this was a notorious area," he recalled.

It has been a long road since then. Besides the discipline and hard work, another thing he learned during his three decades in the army was how to care for people.

"It's not just about barking orders. You must be able to motivate them and show them that you care for them," he said.

"Though training was tough, because we all go through a common training regime, it built strong bonds of friendship, which grows in adversity. This served to establish good networking later in life", he said.

Although he saw the army as a structured and systematic organisation, and that methods of training are constantly evolving to operate new equipment, some basics like discipline and physical fitness will always remain. That, he concluded, is the bedrock of the army.

Although Mr Singh has retired from 'active duty' his best days are still ahead. He believes in leading a healthy lifestyle and his favourite pastimes are taking regular morning walks and playing golf with his former army buddies and old friends. He also bonds with his former colleagues at regular get-to-gathers and most of all enjoying precious time indulging with his grand-children.

BY ABHIJIT NAG

IN A CLASS OF HIS OWN

Velauthur Ambiavagar was not only the first Asian principal of Raffles Institution. He also helped make teaching more rewarding for Singaporeans.

Velauthur Ambiavagar was a man who overcame obstacles. Everything he achieved, he achieved on his own. His determination and passion inspired a generation of students. His commitment was rewarded when he was appointed the first Asian principal of the prestigious school where he had studied and taught, Raffles Institution. As an educator, Ambiavagar was one of the best.

His boyhood years were not easy. Born in Jaffna, Sri Lanka, Ambiavagar lost his mother when he was 11, soon after they moved to Kuala Lumpur in 1916. She left him in the care of his stepbrother, who enrolled him in the Methodist Boys School. While being passionate about sports, he struggled with his studies because his command of English was weak, having begun his schooling in Jaffna in Tamil. Failing his Junior Cambridge examination was perhaps the defining moment of his early life; Ambiavagar refused to be defeated and resolved to study harder.

His diligence paid off when, after coming to Singapore in 1923, he was admitted to Raffles Institution. He passed the School Certificate examination in 1924 and joined the teachers' training course the following year.

In 1928, he entered the newly opened Raffles College on a government scholarship as one of the first batch of 43 students. Graduating in 1931, he was posted to Radin Mas Primary School but a year later began teaching at Raffles Institution. He gave a memorable account of how he got the job. The principal, DW McLeod, questioned him for more than an hour, asking if he would be willing to take charge of various extra-curricular activities. "I finally got annoyed," he later recalled, "and said, 'Look Sir, if I take charge of all these, what would all the other teachers be doing?'"

"Then he smiled and said, 'All right, I like your spirit. I'll have you.'"

A keen sportsman, excelling at cricket, hockey and football, he coached the school's hockey team and led them to many victories.

Within a year of joining Raffles, Ambiavagar was married to Mangaleswary Kandiah on April 15, 1933. His athletic physique and chiselled good looks had always won him admirers, so it was not difficult for him to find a wife. She, like him, was born in Sri Lanka and raised in Malaya, where she had moved with her parents when she was seven. Her childhood was not spent buried in books, like her husband's, but longkang fishing and chasing chickens — quite blissfully. The pair went on to have six children.

Ambiavagar taught at Raffles Institution for 27 years. His natural manner lent itself well to life as an educator, his quiet dignity winning the trust of his students, and his sense of discipline helping him to get the best out of them. His primary interest was always their performance. He believed students should be free thinkers, yet well grounded, if they were to succeed in reforming society and building the nation. Many of his students went on to accomplish great things.

Ambiavagar took pride in their achievements. "I have worn their success in my heart like a gold medal set in precious stones," he said. The influence Ambiavagar had went further than the accomplishments of his students. He began teaching during the colonial era when Asians were considered inferior to colonial Europeans. For example, Asian teachers were made to use separate common rooms from their colonial counterparts, and had much lower salaries and promotion prospects. The separate common rooms at Raffles Institution were abolished after World War II, but other forms of discrimination persisted, favouring expatriates over local teachers. Ambiavagar helped end this discrimination by mobilising his colleagues, presenting key memorandums and negotiating with the colonial government. He helped to make teaching a rewarding profession for Singaporeans.

No one could imagine the changes to come when war broke out. The Ambiavagars had to leave their home in Haig Road when British artillery units took up positions nearby and had to stay with a friend in the McNair Road area.

Everything changed under Japanese Occupation. All classes had to be conducted in Japanese. "I walked to Victoria School to teach Japanese, ate my packed lunch, and walked to St Joseph's Institution to learn the language," Ambiavagar recalled.

In March 1944, he left Singapore with his family, taking a train to Kuala Lumpur to attend to family matters after the death of his sister-in-law and father-in-law. His wife's sister died during childbirth and her father was a victim of Japanese bombing. The family moved into the sister's home in a rural area near Kuala Lumpur. Talking about those days, Ambiavagar later recalled: "I bought some cows and milked them to provide milk for my

Mr Ambiavagar accompanying Sir John Nicoll, Governor of Singapore on Raffles Institution's Founders' Day in 1954.

young children." After the war, the Ambiavagars returned to Singapore. Ambiavagar went back to Raffles Institution and also became a part-time English tutor at Raffles College. He taught there till it became the University of Malaya's arts faculty in 1952.

In his memoirs, he wrote: "My biggest test came early in the post-war years when I was chosen as one of the three delegates to appear before the Governor of Singapore and members of the Executive Council to present the case of all civil servants for back pay for the Japanese Occupation period. I was pushed into the role of leading spokesman because our leader was good at presenting statistics but not at arguing the case and the second guy became tongue-tied in the presence of the high officials. When I started answering questions from the officials, the Governor asked me irrelevantly, "Mr Ambiavagar, I believe you are a Jaffna Tamil?" I had the presence of mind to say, "Yes, Sir, but I don't see what that has to do with our appeal for back pay?" The laughter from the Executive Councillors gave me the courage to answer all subsequent questions fired at me. Whatever, we got the back pay."

He took initiatives in education, too. When the University of Malaya began holding entrance examinations in 1951, he helped launch a three-month Post-Secondary Certificate course at Raffles to prepare students for admission to the university. A year later, the university announced a four-term pre-university course. Eventually, in 1969, the A levels were introduced.

Ambiavagar made another innovation. He introduced Malay in every class at Raffles long before it was made a compulsory subject on the school curriculum, wrote Eugene Wijeysingha in his history of the school, *The Eagle Breeds a Gryphon*. Since there was a shortage of Malay teachers, "Malay boys of higher classes ... were detailed to the various classes to teach while a teacher maintained discipline," he wrote.

In 1953, Ambiavagar became the acting principal of Raffles Institution. He was appointed principal of Beatty Secondary in 1955, but a few months later he was made deputy secretary and deputy director of education.

Finally, in 1958, he became the first Asian principal of Raffles Institution, which was founded more than 100 years ago in 1837. There is a story behind it. "In 1958, because of my trouble with Minister for Education Chew Swee Kee, I was posted back to Raffles Institution as principal," he candidly said in an interview. The minister wanted an Indonesian student, who did not qualify for a place, to be admitted to a local school. When Ambiavagar demurred, he was transferred from the ministry to Raffles. Chew was later impeached for corruption.

Ambiavagar found Raffles lacking in discipline when he returned as principal. He turned out a group of boys who were not making any progress in their studies. When some of the boys tried to make trouble, he made a police report. The boys were let off with a warning and there were no further incidents.

Discipline was restored. "The boys and teachers feared him and trembled at his commands," recalled Wijeysingha, who later became headmaster of the school. "They had the greatest regard for him," he added. He described how, when Ambiavagar later visited the school, "the boys commenced a thunderous applause that could not be calmed, except by Ambiavagar himself."

In 1959, Ambiavagar left Raffles to serve again as deputy director of education. Those were momentous years. On the road to self-governance, Singapore was struggling with the threat of a communist takeover. There were the Chinese middle school riots in 1956. Ambiavagar, who was then Deputy Director of Education, recalled later in an interview: "I advised my director to use some of the newly constructed school buildings as the first government funded Chinese secondary schools in Singapore. We would enrol all students who didn't want to be influenced by the communists." He said: "These were some of the measures taken in the early stages to control communist influences within Chinese schools. It turned out to be very effective."

Ambiavagar also played a leading role in ensuring better opportunities for local teachers. He was chairman of the Singapore Teachers' Association. "When the government introduced legislation that all organisations seeking better wages should be constituted as trade unions,

I took the lead to convert the teachers' association into the Singapore Teachers' Union," he said in an interview.

Following union representations, the government set up a commission to review the salaries of teachers. The commission in its recommendations made a distinction between graduates and other teachers. That was unacceptable to the union and the recommendations were shelved.

However, Ambiavagar raised the issue again. When communists infiltrated the union, he formed the rival Singapore Graduate Teachers' Association. He appealed to the Governor, Sir John Nicoll, to implement the pay commission's recommendations for graduate teachers. Sir John invited him to Government House and said he had decided to implement the salary revision scheme for all teachers. "So we had success in having salaries revised very favourably for local teachers, for graduates as well as non-graduates," said Ambiavagar.

The Singapore education scheme, gazetted in June 1953, was "more than a mere revision of salaries," Ambiavagar noted in his memoirs. "It also raised the status of Asian teachers, giving them equal opportunity with expatriates for promotion to administrative posts and introduced the element of merit for promotion without regard for paper qualification."

Ambiavagar retired as acting permanent secretary and director of education in 1961. It was a defining year for Singapore when Malaya's Prime Minister Tungku Abdul Rahman called for a merger of the two countries, igniting passions that led to a split in the People's Action Party and general elections in 1963. The rigours of overhauling the education system in a society in transition took their toll. Ambiavagar, who had worked under chief ministers David Marshall (1955-56) and Lim Yew Hock (1956-59), called it a day within two years of Prime Minister Lee Kuan Yew's ascent to power. He was under strain. "The long hours he had to put in ... he had to give up many of the activities he enjoyed and another factor that disillusioned him was that it wasn't easy to please his Minister," wrote his wife in her 1996 autobiography, *Three Score and Twenty*.

Mrs Ambiavagar, a former principal of Raffles Girls' Primary and other government schools, was officially honoured as a pioneer educator in 2014 when she celebrated her 100th birthday. Ambiavagar was honoured, too, in his later life. He became an avid golfer after retirement, tutored successive generations of students and wrote a book of short stories called *Easy Money*. Loved and respected by his former students, he celebrated his 90th birthday on October 20, 1995, fêted by the media and his alma maters.

The highlight of the grand occasion was the inauguration of a Raffles Institution scholarship in Ambiavagar's honour, an idea mooted by a longstanding friend, retired teacher Samuel Steven Doraisingham. At the event, the then-president of the Old Rafflesians Association, Dr Chan Peng Mun, paid tribute to Ambiavagar's accomplishments.

The National University of Singapore also paid tribute to Ambiavagar in 1995, when it marked its 90th anniversary with its oldest living alumnus, when he jointly cut the cake with the university's Vice Chancellor, Lim Pin, and the then Prime Minister, Goh Chok Tong.

Ambiavagar died on January 10, 2002, at the age of 96.

He was a man who worked hard for success, and whose strong values were at the heart of everything he did. Mrs Ambiavagar, who affectionately called her husband "Ambi", phrased it thus in her memoir: "Most events in Ambi's life happened by accident. Even if he did not plan the events of his life, he really made a good job of every one of them."

BY ABHIJIT NAG

BRINGING THE NEWS

Ananda Perera was the man behind the news on television from the 1980s till the early 1990s.

It was show time for him everyday when people tuned into the English news. He had scrutinised every nut and bolt of news production from the filming, reporting and editing to the makeup and clothes of the newsreaders. Ministers would also be intently watching the reporters and newsreaders presenting what the Government wanted the people to know. He was the man in charge and responsible for what went on air.

Ananda Perera was director of news from 1982 to 1992, at the Singapore Broadcasting Corporation (SBC), which later became MediaCorp.

"He had very high standards for the newsroom," recalled a former colleague when he passed away in 2011. Trained by the BBC, Perera learned on the job. He was a veteran who got into television even before Singapore became a nation. Before that, he was a teacher.

He had the greatest admiration for Lee Kuan Yew, said his wife. Lalitha Perera, his wife of 48 years, smiled as she recalled him as a teenager. "He was the heart-throb of several girls in our small Sinhala community. He was so handsome and serious! But he preferred the company of books and discussing the teachings of the Lord Buddha with monks to girl-watching!" Well, he did look at her, and she at him. "We were teenage sweethearts," she said. "Our two families were friends," she explained. "We met often in the Sri Lankaramaya Buddhist temple at St Michael's Road."

Born on May 16, 1929, Perera came from a deeply religious family. His maternal grandfather, APM Daniel, who came from Ceylon (now Sri Lanka), did two things on arriving in Singapore. He set up Lanka Hotel, at Trafalgar Street in Tanjong Pagar, catering mainly to young Sinhalese men from Ceylon. More significantly, he set up the first Theravada Buddhist temple on the island.

One of the young visitors, a high-caste Buddhist like Daniel, Morawakage S Perera was a telegraphist who later worked for the *Malay Tribune*. He married Daniel's eldest daughter. The couple had four children; the two older boys survived while the younger two died during the war years. Ananda was their second son. His full name was Morawakage Rupananda Perera, but he shortened it to Ananda Perera. Fortune smiled on his mother when she conceived him. She won $10,000 in a lottery. The windfall relieved a burden. Her father had mortgaged their Outram Road property to build their first temple to accommodate the growing Buddhist population. Happily, she used half her winnings to pay off the mortgage.

A bright boy, he suffered from asthma in childhood. But his grandfather, a horoscope reader, predicted that he would one day serve famous people. In his formative years, he stayed in Ceylon where he and his brother learned music, poetry and Buddhism. As young boys, he and his brother sang spiritual songs during Vesak Day for Radio Singapore.

After attending Outram Primary School, he was admitted to Raffles Institution in 1952. Elated, his parents planned a dinner celebration, but it was not to be. His father suddenly died of heart failure. His mother was unable to run the hotel she had managed with her husband since her father's death. Perera matured overnight. He was to become his mother's right hand, even helping in domestic chores. In spite of achieving high grades from Raffles Institution in 1956, and doing Special Papers in English literature, he opted to work for the income tax department for about a year. Then he joined the Teachers' Training College (TTC) at Paterson Road, where he earned as he learned, instead of

He down-graded his teaching position to a floor manager, only to rise to the top job in the news division. That was his inimitable character always taking challenges.

attending university. He also completed a course at Dale Carnegie's. At 19, he represented Singapore at the Southeast Asia seminar of the American Friends Service Committee (Quakers) in Ceylon.

In 1960, he first taught in primary schools before his transfer to Cedar Girls' Secondary School. His sterling performance attracted the attention of officials from the Ministry of Education.

In September 1963, he married Lalitha Fernando after he broke up an engagement arranged by his mother. She was an undergraduate then, reading English and geography at the University of Singapore.

"There were ignorant others who talked about our caste differences," she recalled. "He was a true Buddhist believing what Lord Buddha said, that your caste is your character. Even then, he had spiritual powers of introspection. His mother and my parents blessed our marriage as he was bent on marrying me.

"We lived with his mother for a few years. She helped me look after my son, Sanjay," said Mrs Perera, who later had twin daughters, Yasodha and Yamuna. "She returned to Sri Lanka (where her eldest son lived) and passed on after an illness."

"Marrying him was my greatest achievement in life!" said Mrs Perera. Thin and delicate, with a wave of her hand, she dismissed the fact that he never went to university. "I was enjoying a very comfortable life, while he was the proverbial salmon swimming upstream. I greatly admired him. I thought he was a wonderful teacher. I also wanted to become a teacher so that we would have holidays together.

"As a teenager, Ananda used to save his 20 cents' bus fare money and walked to Bras Basah Road to buy second-hand books," she recalled. "The National Library was his saviour and that is how he gleaned a great deal of knowledge. He did not need paper qualifications.

"Ananda assisted me in my studies, especially in English literature, as he was a prolific reader and taught me how to write essays for my Certificate in Education at the TTC," she added.

Mrs Perera taught for 20 years at St Joseph's Convent, her alma mater. Later, she served as head of the English Department and vice-principal at government secondary schools.

Perera gave up teaching soon after marriage. In 1963, when television came to Singapore, he was invited by the Ministry of Education to apply for a job with educational TV services for schools.

When he went for the interview, however, the Public Service Commission Chairman, Cheng Tong Fatt, wanted him to work on contract as a floor manager at Radio and Television Singapore (RTS) instead.

"It meant giving up his permanent job as a teacher and a civil servant. I was flabbergasted," says Mrs Perera. "But he said he knew what he was doing. That was his inimitable character — always taking challenges!" When Cheng Tong Fatt later became chairman of SBC, he was proud of his protégé for his remarkable success.

The racial riots that broke out soon after he joined television were a nightmare in 1964. Mrs Perera recalled, "We were living with his mother in a rented bungalow in Upper Serangoon when the riots broke out. The Ministry of Defence told all principals to send their teachers and students home. Military trucks came to take us home. On reaching home, I heard that Ananda had called to say that he would be staying overnight at the TV station. I couldn't even talk to him. I saw him only the next day late in the evening."

When Singapore broke away from Malaysia in 1965, Lee Kuan Yew cried during the inaugural speech on Channel 5. Perera was the floor manager during that momentous occasion. The Prime Minister wanted the scene to be cut off, but the cameras rolled and later a collective decision was made with the authorities to show it. Ever since, that TV clip has been played many times.

A thorough professional, Perera showed both talent and dedication. His documentaries won the Asian Broadcasting Union awards three times. In 1973, he was sent to the U.K. to be trained by the BBC. Setting a high premium on education, he recommended several producers to get university degrees. They remember him for being a stickler for punctuality and never procrastinating on any job.

He had a very stressful job as director of news. "Ananda always received phone calls from Ministers regarding news items as they were keen to have their activities televised," said Mrs Perera. "He was meticulous when Ministers were televised. In the studio, he helped with articulation of words, how to face the camera and pick clothes of the right colour. He was very upfront but so caring that they obliged."

Important occasions like National Day Parades and Prime Minister's speeches meant more work. He produced the first National Day Parades, National Day Rally speeches, live broadcast and the funerals of two Presidents, Yusof Ishak and Benjamin Sheares.

"He worked his guts out as he had to please the Ministers. He worked into the wee hours of the morning for productions at Caldecot Hill and meetings at the Istana. I used to be upset, sitting up and waiting for him," Mrs Perera recalled. "He went through the speeches meticulously as he wanted to prepare the camera angles. He constantly checked on productions and the newsreaders and called them up immediately when he wasn't happy."

He was fun-loving, too, and enjoyed going to the movies with his family, driving to Malaysia and cooking. A popular singer of Hindi and Tamil songs, he sang at community concerts, temples and for Malay and Indian TV programmes. He also played the tabla.

Perera became director of public affairs after serving as director of news. He retired in 1995 after more than 30 years in television.

He continued watching news programmes but thought newscasters had become more concerned about their hair and clothes. A regular writer to *The Straits Times* Forum page, he even wrote about a newscaster wearing black on New Year's Day.

He died of pneumonia after a battle with lung cancer on September 28, 2011.

"I have stopped watching TV since Ananda left. I have other meaningful activities," said Mrs Perera, who lives with her son. She visits cancer patients at home and in Sri Lanka, goes for long walks, reads, writes, paints, meditates, tends her garden and attends lectures at the Theosophical Society. She is also in the temple committee trying to save the first Theravada temple, in Outram Road, from being sold. In between, she visits her daughters, in the U.K. and Australia. Her husband's photo albums, copious love letters and songs on audio cassettes and CDs evoke precious memories. He is only "a heartbeat away", she says, as she connects with him spiritually and is back with the man she continues to love.

BY VEENA BHARWANI

STAMPING HIS MARK

Singapore's first Singaporean postmaster general, Bala Supramanion, talks about the Japanese Occupation forces, silent movies and one-cent coffee.

In a world dominated by email and the internet, it is hard to imagine a time when every letter had to be written on paper and most were sent out by post. That was the domain of M Bala Supramanion. He was the first Singaporean to be the postmaster general in 1967. Bala started working for the General Post Office in 1936 and continued during the Japanese Occupation, when he learned to speak Japanese fluently. Contrary to the views held by most other Singaporeans, he was impressed by the occupying forces and their occupation had a profound influence on the youngster.

The 97-year-old spoke gently about the harsh realities of working for the occupying forces. According to him, the Japanese rarely smiled and were very strict, and the Postal and Telegraph Services were very strategic to them as it was their only means of communication.

"They set an officious tone in the workplace and imposed strict standards of discipline. Senior officers, who were demanding and their authority unquestionable, imposed high standards of obedience, discipline and loyalty on their Japanese subordinates as well," he recalled. Kindness was not in their blood. The Japanese were uncompromising to those who failed in their tasks, unsympathetic to those unable to keep deadlines, and never hesitated to mete out harsh punishment to malingerers.

However, Bala recounted with a touch of pride his admiration for the Japanese work ethics when he was a teenager, despite the perceived harshness.

"They placed a greater commitment to the greater cause they were working or fighting for. As a youngster, I was influenced by their doctrines and these qualities shaped my thinking, which I would later apply in my career. I became more resourceful and understood the value of discipline and commitment," he said.

Supramanion in a bow-tie at a staff function. In the background is a youthful Lee Kuan Yew who would emerge as the world's youngest and Singapore's first Prime Minister.

While we celebrate his achievements, we also recognise that Bala was born in a Singapore that no longer exists today. We pause and admire what he has seen in the past and what he continues to see in an ever-changing Singapore.

Born in the sleepy confines of Potong Pasir in 1917, Bala amused himself as a boy rearing fighting fishes, admiring their colours, and provocativeness as they taunted each other. "We kept them in separate bottles, to prevent them from nipping each other," he reminisced.

During the dry season, he played marbles on parched grounds and watched spinning tops on scorched sandy pitches When the windy season came, he launched his kite for aerial battles with other kites, slicing glass-coated strings, sending the vanquished wandering in the drifting winds.

There were no street lights and electricity. People at home lit hurricane lamps as darkness fell. Others sat outdoors beneath the pale moonlight. In the stillness of the night, they watched silent movies before sound was dubbed onto movies in the late 1920s. "We sat on both sides of the transparent screen. It was cheaper to watch movies from the opposite (reverse) side, which cost one cent for a movie," said Bala.

Pictures were shown in the open and there was the orchestra playing music to dramatise scenes in cinema halls.

"Nowadays it is so difficult to buy tickets for a movie. You have to call to book your seats. Then, you were asked whether you wanted a 'couple seat' or 'love seat' ".

The gentle soul spoke about a Singapore that was very different from what it is now.

"As a young boy, I used to witness bullock carts towing away sand for construction from Potong Pasir. People lived in villages, kampongs. Commuted by trams (on tracks), trolley buses and rickshaws; bullock-carts. Cars were owned by towkays and British. Rickshaw pullers had a particular dress code. Loose shirt, three-quarter pants, huge hat to protect from the sun. Shoes were made from cut tyres. Even half a cent coin had value.

"Ten cents could buy you a vegetarian meal and coffee cost one cent. Half a cup of coffee cost half a cent. There were no facilities at home. Firewood was used for cooking and we collected water from stand pipes for free or from ponds and wells."

He said he was taught how to survive and stressed how, unlike his generation, the young today would not be able to survive without amenities.

As Singapore celebrates its 50th year of independence, Bala marvels at the progress made in the last 30 years. He never expected to see such progress. Singapore has been transformed from an under-developed country into a first-world nation in a very short time. "Historically, no country has developed as fast as Singapore. It took Europe centuries," he said.

He believes we owe all our success to Lee Kuan Yew. "He was the key leader who had the ability to choose people to assist him — people like Goh Keng Swee, Rajaratnam, Toh Chin Chye, Eddie Barker and Othman Wok who brought all the races together," he said.

Other figures also helped to make Singapore what it is today. Lee Kuan Yew helped to set up the Industrial Development Board to attract industries to Singapore. The Housing Development Board was set up for the poor, not for the rich.

"Lee Kuan Yew will be an icon of inspiration for the new generation," he affirmed.

Singapore's first President, Yusof Ishak, being conducted around the mail-sorting section at General Post Office by Director of Posts M Bala Supramanion in April 1961.

Yusof Ishak Collection, Courtesy of National Archives of Singapore

BY VEENA BHARWANI

BREAKING THE MOULD

Balbir Kaur is the first woman to serve as a regimental sergeant major in Singapore. It's a challenging role for a girl who was encouraged by her dad to join the air force.

I t's not easy being a woman in a man's world, especially when you have to train and discipline soldiers. Just ask Balbir Kaur, the first warrant officer in the Singapore Armed Forces to take on the role of regimental sergeant major. It is hard to imagine the soft-spoken lady assuming such a post. She is proud of the honour, however, and is grateful to her commanders for giving her such a "challenging role".

Even though she's now a senior warrant officer expected to maintain standards and discipline, she recalls a carefree childhood.

"We used to stay in Kampong Eunos," she said. "We had a nice big house with lots of open spaces to play and lots of fruit trees. There was this one guava tree that I loved to climb, and everyone knew where to find me if I had gone missing. My dad was quite strict with us kids, especially in our bearing. He would always remind us not to slouch, to stand tall, stomach in, chest out and so on. We had Chinese, Malay and Indian neighbours, so all the kids used to play together."

"During the kampong days," she added, "we had lots of fun flying kites, riding bicycles, playing 'bola hentam', catching fish in the drains and anything else that we came up with. As I grew older, I played badminton and took up reading."

As she grew up, she was drawn to a career in the armed forces, thanks to her father. "I joined the service in late 1978," she said. "My family, particularly my dad, was instrumental in me joining the Republic of Singapore Air Force (RSAF). He used to work for the RAF (Royal Air Force) as an administrative staff and had a very high regard for military service. He felt a military career would build character and be a good career choice for me. I applied and was selected after the first round of interviews. I also met my husband in the RSAF, and

I must say he is the pillar who has always been there for me and supported me in all my decisions."

She remembered things were very different back in the early days. "Things were slower paced. The systems we had were a legacy from the RAF. I remembered working 8 to 5 then, but this slowly changed to 24/7 operations to meet our defence needs. Over the years, I have seen the RSAF transform from a first-generation to a third-generation force with cutting-edge technology."

Her unprecedented appointment to what used to be a man's job has not gone unnoticed. The MINDEF newsletter, *Cyber Pioneer*, turned the spotlight on her in 2007 when it reported: "After being in the air force for 27 years, the most memorable experience for Master Warrant Officer Balbir Kaur, Officer Commanding, Air Operations Systems Specialist Training Flight, came in 2000 when she was appointed regimental sergeant major."

"In this appointment, you have to be good in operations," she told the reporter. "You also have to deal with men on the ground, and deal with regimentation, discipline and taking on parades. That was quite challenging for me. "I think I have excelled," she added, "but we can only be successful with the support and belief of our commanders and the men on the ground."

She remembered being thanked by a complete stranger who praised the air force. This was after an incident in 2008 when the RSAF detected a Cessna aircraft, which had travelled all the way from the north without a flight plan.

"The Cessna," she said, "was intercepted by our F-16s and escorted to land in Changi Airport uneventfully. This incident reminded us that we must always be vigilant to ensure the integrity of our airspace is maintained 24 hours a day, seven days a week. This news was published in *The Straits Times* and several other newspapers. A couple of days later, while I was on my way home after work, a male Singaporean approached me and asked if I was in the air force. I said yes, and he applauded the RSAF for a job well done and thanked me for my service to the country."

Balbir is among an expanding brigade of women who dare to be different.

She does the same job as the male regimental sergeant majors. Besides maintaining discipline and regimentation in her unit, she is involved in parades at the unit level as well as on big occasions such as the National Day. As an air operations systems specialist, she also functions as a primary operations controller who has to ensure operation standards are maintained by the servicemen. She does not believe in top-down management, preferring to both listen and talk to the servicemen.

Don't let her quiet demeanour fool you. When push comes to shove, she can be stern with the men.

"One of my biggest challenges," she said as a regimental sergeant major in an interview with *Air Force News* several years ago, "was to overcome the fear of taking parades." However, she gained self-confidence after training non-SAF contingents for the National Day Parade and undergoing the army battalion regimental sergeant-major's course.

A seasoned veteran, she is now helping prepare her juniors. "In my current capacity as a section head in the Air Training Department," she said, "I am responsible for the training roadmaps for the development of our RSAF warrant officers, specialists, and military experts."

"My tour has been enriching," she added. "What I have learned over the years is that the SAF/RSAF is an organisation that provides many opportunities for us to develop ourselves to our fullest potential — and if that opportunity knocks on your door, take it. My wish is to continue to serve the RSAF well and be the best I can be."

BY ABHIJIT NAG

BROADCAST GURU

Pioneer broadcaster S Chandra Mohan
"helped me get my views across",
said the late Prime Minister Lee Kuan Yew.

S Chandra Mohan was a pioneer of the broadcast industry in Singapore and over his career spanning five decades, he served in key executive positions in the industry, initiated and developed many current affairs programmes and nurtured several generations of broadcasts journalists and documentary producers. Near the start of his long career, he was the TV news producer who directed the coverage of the historic TV press conference which announced that Singapore had been forced out of Malaysia. His instructions to the cameraman resulted in the now famous image of Prime Minister Lee Kuan Yew's emotional moment on that historic day in 1965.

Chandra Mohan's lasting legacy — the development of broadcast journalism in Singapore — was acknowledged when he died on 28th August 2010, aged 71. Singapore's first Prime Minister Lee Kuan Yew wrote in a condolence letter dated 30 August 2010 to Mrs Nirmala Chandra Mohan, where he stated, "He was most capable and helped me get my views across, first on radio, then on television, during all the years I was Prime Minister. He was highly intelligent and competent."

Of the coverage of Lee's historical TV conference after Singapore was forced out of Malaysia in 1965. Lee noted, "I had to stop halfway because I could not control my emotions. He decided to show part of it. From the feedback I got, he made the right decision."

Chandra Mohan joined the Singapore Broadcasting Corporation as a producer in 1962. The working relationship between Lee and Chandra Mohan (known to his friends and colleagues as "Chandra") lasted throughout Chandra's career.

Prime Minister Lee Hsien Loong also shared this trust of Chandra's experience and guidance, in his condolence letter to Mrs Chandra Mohan on 30th August, 2010, saying:

"He distilled long, complex political debates into 45 minutes of watchable television and made sure they were coherent and balanced.

"I remember one studio discussion that had gone well, and overrun the targeted time. I remarked to Chandra that it would be hard to compress the material since all seemed relevant. But with his greater experience he replied that by looking closely at the transcript, he would identify sections to edit out, which would tighten and improve the programme. Of course, he was right. It was a pleasure working with him."

It was no surprise then that his memory is treasured by various Cabinet ministers.

Minister Vivian Balakrishnan said, "My father and I have known him for many decades. We used to live nearby; he used to walk past our house. For me, I've known him through my years debating and participating in various current affairs shows. He's always been a very nice man, a good source of advice."

He held key positions within the then Singapore Broadcasting Corporation, playing a pivotal role in the station's programmes and driving award-winning shows, such as Diary of a Nation.

He was also instrumental in the launch of Radio Singapore International in 1994. "He showed me everything from how to tell a story, how to peel the layers of stories and the most instrumental — how to manage national programmes," recalled one of his former colleagues Tan Lek Hwa, former vice-president, English Current Affairs, MediaCorp.

Arun Mahizhnan, Special Research Adviser at the Institute of Policy Studies at the National University of Singapore, was a former colleague of Chandra's. He had worked for him for 10 years in the Central Productions Unit.

Arun said, "Chandra was part of the first generation of pure breed of television journalists. Despite having no prior experience in the print or broadcast media, he demonstrated a grasp of the medium that was exceptional.

He strove for excellence and would not settle for mediocrity, bringing a level of intelligence and sense of aesthetics that were rare those days. He also laid the foundation for new formats, like documentaries, current affairs forums, and weekly magazines.

I joined the Central Production Unit (CPU) partly because of him, even though I had other options in Radio and Television Singapore (RTS). I wanted to train under him and work for him as I was much impressed by his reputation. It turned out be the best decision I made in my broadcasting life.

Contrary to many civil servants of that time, he did not stand on ceremony or protocol. Everyone could call him "Chandra" instead of "Mr Chandra Mohan" the common practice of the time. It also symbolised the way he treated his staff – as colleagues rather than as subordinates. He was insistent that we have to keep learning from other sources — as he was doing himself. He plied the staff with numerous articles and broadcast journals and frequently analysed foreign programmes with staff. It was a great learning experience for me. In effect, he was my primary television guru and writing coach. He had a wonderful way with words and relished good writing."

Ramesh Panicker, executive producer and writer, recalled, "Chandra was director of Current Affairs in the then Singapore Broadcasting Corporation when I joined the division fresh out of university. I'd be lying if I said I wasn't intimidated by him. His reputation as a broadcaster preceded him. I found him a serious, incisive, intense, intelligent man who produced great work — especially in the documentary genre."

Mrs Nirmala Chandra Mohan, his wife, remarked on the extent to which Chandra cared for his family. "He was a devoted father to Arjuna and Shakuntala, always sensitive to their needs," she said. "Despite his busy schedule, he spent quality time with them without fail. Every Sunday morning he would go swimming with them. He enjoyed that very much.

"He was a filial son. When we got married, Chandra let me know that it was important to him that we stay with his aged parents as he wanted to look after them. Beyond providing a beautiful home for us and his parents, he instituted a Sunday lunch dedicated to his parents, leaving always the choice of dishes to them.

"He was a loving and kind husband," said Mrs Chandra Mohan. "Living with him was an education itself. Through generously sharing the learning which he had achieved in his drama and film experience with me, I entered a new world of creativity and sensitivity. We used to watch four movies a day before the children were born. I just used to watch the storyline but after having married Chandra I learnt about direction, production, lighting and the qualities of the best actors and directors He introduced me to Satyajit Ray, Akira Kurosawa, Alfred Hitchcock, Oliver Stone and others. These artistic and intellectual hobbies of his bonded us. It gives me great joy even now to watch a movie and think about Chandra's appreciation of the arts."

His series of documentaries were popular among Singaporeans and his techniques of dramatising scenes and shots laid foundations for others to follow.

His daughter, Shakuntala remarked that Chandra's discipline and dedication to his work set a fine example for her. She remembers him working long hours during events such as the National Day Rally, his fine penmanship and his great attention to the detail. Arjuna was inspired by these characteristics as well as the great loyalty which Chandra inspired in the people who worked with him. Many had commented to the family that Chandra was the sort of person who took on great pressure, excelled in producing results and at the same time, made the people around him feel respected and cared for.

Marc Dass, Chandra Mohan's nephew, said, "Even now, when I watch the documentaries on Singapore politics, I remember what he shared and his involvement and influential role as a member of the media in capturing the human elements that shaped and occurred in our country's history. Chandra was a kind uncle with firm beliefs and strong values, which he held in his personal and professional life."

Jacinta Stephens, a former SBC/Television Corporation of Singapore (TCS) current affairs producer and documentaries editor said, "Chandra could be considered the father of broadcast journalism here. He mentored and nurtured several generations of broadcast journalists and documentary producers, bringing an intellectual vigor and great passion to the profession.

"He was there at or almost from the start of Singapore's television days and was instrumental in shaping broadcast journalism as it evolved here. He was there to record, analyse, report and later oversee many milestone events and issues from Separation from Malaysia to the various live telecasts of election results and the annual prime minister's rally speech.

"One of the things that really helped me personally and my career was his high standards. He was willing to consider new ideas, fresh perspectives. He respected those of us who dared to challenge him. He could spot talent — he could tell a news hound from a deep documentaries type — and gave us room to grow. He would look at the empty seats in the office and say that was a good thing. He reckoned if we were sitting around, then we were probably not doing it right. He expected us to be out there, really getting into the bloodstream of issues and events. It also helped that he had a great wit, sense of humour and fun.

"He was an intellectual through and through. Had a passion for books and documentaries and even after his retirement and through his illness, he would be reading several books concurrently and watching documentaries with a critical eye. With him will die a rich treasure trove of stories and analysis about Singapore, its leaders, its politics and its evolution. Personally, I will miss my mentor and the bright, rich and deep conversations. I am grateful for so much that he taught us."

BY ABHIJIT NAG

SHOTS UNDER FIRE

His pictures continue to tell their own story long after Chellappah Canagaratnam became the first Singaporean photographer to die in the Vietnam war.

The first Singaporean photographer to die in the Vietnam war, Chellappah Canagaratnam was only 25. The young man, who died only five months after Singapore became a new nation, is remembered to this day, 50 years later. A daredevil, he loved climbing coconut trees as a boy, recalled his elder brother, C Tharalingam, 80. Always looking for adventure, Chellappah wasn't cut out for a nine-to-five job. With a camera around his neck, he went from place to place, filing news photos. Travelling around the region, he wound up in in the war zone. On January 21, 1965, he arrived in Saigon, now Ho Chi Minh City. A year later he was dead, killed in a landmine blast.

But his pictures survive. Pulitzer-winning photo journalist Horst Faas, under whom he worked for the Associated Press in Vietnam, featured him in a book called *Requiem*, about photographers who died in Vietnam and Indochina.

Faas, wounded in the war himself in 1967, was struck by the young man's fearlessness. His close-up shots of combat and casualties were so dramatic that Faas warned him to be more careful. But Chellappah, nicknamed Charlie by the Americans, wanted to be in the thick of the action. Faas, who saw his final shots, could only marvel at his courage. "The pictures show, better than any words could, how close Chellappah was to the action up to the moment of his death," he wrote in *Requiem*.

Two other Singaporean photographers, Terence Khoo and Sam Kai Faye, died in the war. They were out together in a battle zone when they were killed by enemy fire on July 21, 1972. Both had once worked for *The Straits Times*.

Chellappah was killed on Valentine's Day. Love might have been in the air elsewhere, but February 14, 1966, was another terrible day in a treacherous place so sinister that the Americans called it Hell's Half Acre. Crawling with the enemy, bristling with hidden landmines, the place threatened death at every step. A stronghold of Viet Cong guerrillas, who hid in its tunnels, Cu Chi — that was its real name — was a danger zone just north-west of Saigon. Nerves on edge, American soldiers were there on a road-clearing mission when a Viet Cong claymore mine went off. Chellappah, who was with the soldiers, went to the rescue of the wounded, but a second mine killed them all.

His family heard about his death in a Tamil news bulletin on Radio Singapore. *The Associated Press* arranged for the body to be flown back. The family cremated the body and scattered the ashes in the sea off Bedok.

A month after the funeral came a letter from the deceased. Yes, his body was brought home before his letter arrived. It showed the young man had been thinking of home and his own life. He was planning to go to Hong Kong, he wrote, and to buy medical insurance for himself.

Cu Chi is now a tourist destination. Visitors can see the narrow, claustrophobic tunnels, which have been turned into a memorial park. The Vietnamese honour the dead just like the Americans with their Vietnam Veterans Memorial in Washington, DC. The memories refuse to go away.

Chellappah's pictures saw the light of day again when *Requiem*, the book, was published in 1997. The book led to a travelling exhibition, also called *Requiem*, showing the works of the photographers killed in Vietnam. His were among the pictures shown when the exhibition touched these shores in 2011.

It offered some consolation to his family. His sister, C Parameswari, contacted *The Straits Times* after reading that the exhibition was coming to Singapore. The newspaper put her in touch with Tim Page, the British war photographer who edited the book with Faas.

Chellapah's passion for adventure drove him to the battlefields of Vietnam.

The harrowing pictures bore witness to Chellappah's courage. So did the accompanying words at the exhibition, which noted: "Chellappah's bravery was what led him to follow American GIs on February 14, 1966 to Cu Chi, north-west of Saigon — a place which was also known as Hell's Half Acre, because of the number of people killed in that dangerous, dense jungle rubber plantation littered with Vietcong tunnels and camouflaged with snipers."

Parameswari told *The Straits Times* there had been 10 siblings in their Sri Lankan family and their father was the City Council water district supervisor. Chellappah's search for adventure led him to be as a freelance photographer and sports writer for the *Singapore Free Press*. He later moved to Kuala Lumpur, where he joined the Malayan Times. Subsequently, he went to work for the *Sabah Daily Express* before the Vietnam war beckoned when he was in Hong Kong. His elder brother, C Tharmalingam, said he was "driven by a strong sense of purpose and was destined to be at the heart of the action, and the battle ground seemed to him where the action was".

He attended Monk's Hill Primary as a child and completed his secondary education at Gan Eng Seng. Added Tharmalingam: "He was a selfless person who always put others before himself, whether it was his school mates, colleagues or comrades. It was this commitment to work and friendship that claimed his life. Unfortunately, his courage was his misfortune."

"I thank my stars that the exhibition came to Singapore," said Parameswari. "Now finally my brother has got back his name again." His funeral, held at his family's home in Jalan Kesembi, Woodlands, was attended by many. Tim Page, who curated *Requiem*, said he was also grateful for the sense of closure it brought Chellappah's family, The exhibition, he added, was the best thing he had ever done in his life.

Interviews: C. Tharmalingam; C.Thillagaratnam
Bibliography: Vietnam: Why We Fought
An Illustrated History: Dorothy & Thomas Hoobler
The Tunnels of Cu Chi: Tom Mangold and John Penycate Requiem

The Straits Times 6 August '04 pg. H13

BY ABHIJIT NAG

THE UNIONIST

The only PAP member to be elected to Parliament in both Singapore and Malaysia, former President Devan Nair helped create a business-friendly climate.

He had the rare honour of being elected by the voters of two countries. The only People's Action Party (PAP) member to be elected to the Malaysian parliament, C V Devan Nair was subsequently recalled to Singapore, where he won a parliamentary seat before being elected the third President of the new nation. "Given my temperament, perhaps the greatest error I ever made in my life was to accept appointment as President of Singapore," he rued after relinquishing office in unfortunate circumstances.

His later life was clouded by controversy, but there is no denying his role as a nation builder. "During the formative years of our nation, he served with courage and commitment, and played a significant part in building modern Singapore," said Prime Minister Lee Hsien Loong in a condolence letter to his family following his death on December 6, 2005.

Devan Nair played a crucial role as a union leader. As a founder and the first secretary-general of the National Trades Union Congress (NTUC), he promoted good relations between workers and management, creating a business-friendly climate which helped Singapore flourish. This was acknowledged by then Prime Minister Lee Kuan Yew, who wanted Nair to be President. "Because he wanted to do something about the sufferings and deprivations of the people, he became a tower of strength in our battles against the communists and communalists. It needed fortitude to cease playing the hero strike leader and instead to re-educate the workers, to reshape their attitudes towards management, from a confrontational to a cooperational one," he said, speaking on the motion to elect Nair as President on October 23, 1981.

Nair could reach out to the workers as a unionist who had stood on picket lines and slept on the gravel with them as a former militant who had done time in colonial prisons.

The third President of Singapore had been a communist sympathizer before he became a follower of Lee.

Born in Malacca on 5 August 1923, he was the son of a rubber plantation clerk, an immigrant from Kerala in India, who brought the family to Singapore when Nair was 10 years old. The boy attended Rangoon Road Primary School and Victoria School, passing the Senior Cambridge examination in 1940. After the Second World War, Nair became a teacher and taught at St Andrew's School. Drawn into the trade union movement, he became the general secretary of the Singapore Teachers' Union.

He also joined the Anti-British League — in his own words, "an underground auxiliary of the Malayan Communist Party" — and fell afoul of the colonial authorities. In 1951, he was detained on St John's Island, where he spent the next two years, for his speeches against colonial rule and in favour of communist revolution.

Later, he wrote: "I look back nostalgically to my years of incarceration, for they were years of intensive reading and self-education."

It was at "St John's University", as he called it, that he met Lee Kuan Yew, who helped the detainees as a lawyer.

In 1953, he married Dhanalatchimi, whom he had known since childhood as her brother's friend; but life was no bed of roses. He was not allowed to be a school teacher when he was released from detention. To make ends meet, he had to give private tuition for about $80 a month. Undaunted, he resumed union activities and in 1954 became a founder member of the People's Action Party.

Mr Devan Nair at AUPE Annual Delegates' Conference flanked by G. Kandasamy AUPE General Secretary and Ow Kheng Thor, Deputy General Secretary.

Mr Devan Nair chatting with local and overseas unionists at NTUC's First Annual Delegates' Conference held in 1962.

In 1956, he was again detained with other unionists following riots triggered by strikes. He was released in 1959 when the PAP won the general election; the PAP refused to take office until the British freed the unionists. That was when Nair renounced communism in signed statements as urged by Lee, the new Prime Minister.

In 1961, the pro-communists split from the PAP, which sought independence for Singapore through merger with Malaysia. The pro-communists formed Barisan Sosialis and their followers broke away from the Singapore Trade Union Congress to set up the Singapore Association of Trade Unions (SATU). Most of the unions joined SATU. PAP loyalists like Devan Nair had to create an alternative. They formed the National Trades Union Congress on September 6, 1961.

The PAP got the better of its opponents and Singapore became part of Malaysia in 1963. But when the PAP contested the Malaysian general election in 1964, Devan Nair was the only PAP candidate to win a seat. Elected from Bungsar, near Kuala Lumpur, he remained in Malaysia — where he formed the Democratic Action Party — when Singapore became independent in 1965.

His wife and children, however, returned to Singapore just three days after independence on August 9, 1965. His wife, elected to the Singapore state legislature in 1963, became a member of the new Parliament. "My siblings and I suddenly found ourselves with a set of parents, each of whom was a member of a different national legislature, sworn to defend a different nation," recalled Janamitra Devan, the couple's second son, years later. "It was an absurd situation; it couldn't last; it didn't."

Mr Devan Nair attending the National Trade Union Congress First Annual Delegates Conference in 1962.

Nair was recalled to Singapore by Lee to lead the NTUC. It was a time of high unemployment when labour laws had to be revamped to attract investors and create new jobs. Nair chaired the NTUC Modernization Seminar, which inspired new co-operatives and stressed the need for workers to cooperate with the government and the employers so they could all benefit from economic growth.

In 1979, Nair was elected MP for Anson in a by-election. He retained the seat in the 1980 general election but gave it up the following year. On October 23, 1981, he was elected President by Parliament. This led to another by-election at Anson, which was won by JB Jeyaretnam, the first opposition candidate to win a seat in Parliament since independence.

Nair later complained Lee "kicked me upstairs". It was, he said, "the silliest job in the world. All you had to do was cut ribbons." He didn't last a full term. He stepped down on March 28, 1985, seven months before due, after a visit to Sarawak.

Lee told Parliament that Nair "developed symptoms of extreme weakness and exhaustion associated with mental confusion and bizarre behaviour" in Sarawak and had to be brought back to Singapore. Medical examination revealed he was "was suffering from an acute confusional state due to alcohol superimposed on a long-standing condition caused by alcohol dependency".

Nair went to New York for treatment. He was offered a pension of $5,000 a month provided he was regularly checked by a panel of government doctors. He declined the offer, saying it meant spending his last years "under a cloud".

Three years later, he left Singapore. He went to the United States and in 1995 moved to Hamilton, near Toronto, in Canada.

The former President became a fierce critic of Lee in his retirement years, leading to an acrimonious lawsuit that Lee rebutted with a counter lawsuit.

Nair died in Hamilton, Ontario, on December 6, 2005, nearly eight months after losing his wife. She died in a Hamilton hospital on April 18, 10 days after contracting pneumonia. She was 80 years old. Nair was 82.

Prime Minister Lee Hsien Loong, Lee Kuan Yew and other leaders paid their respects at a memorial service in Singapore on January 7, 2006. Lim Boon Heng, the then NTUC secretary-general, said in his speech: "Devan Nair was the founder of modern trade unionism in Singapore. Today the enduring values of our trade union movement are largely the same as his. Like him, we uphold the values of fairness at work, and social justice in society at large. Like him, we are pragmatic, not ideological, in our approach to achieving our goals."

Now the NTUC has founded an adult education centre and named it in his honour. The Devan Nair Institute for Employment and Employability was launched by Lee Hsien Loong, who said: "It is fitting that this institute is named after Mr Devan Nair. He was one of our pioneer union leaders who built up the non-communist union movement, served as sec-gen for many years and was pivotal in forging a united and forward-looking labour movement."

"In more ways than one, this is a homecoming," said Janadas Devan, Nair's eldest son, the chief of government communications. Though the former President lies buried in a grave in Hamilton, Singapore is keeping his memory alive.

Mr Devan addressing the first Public Services International Seminar in May 1964.

BY ABHIJIT NAG

THE NATIONAL BARD

There is the public Edwin Thumboo and the private Edwin Thumboo. One writes for the nation, but who is closer to the reader?

E dwin Thumboo is widely regarded as the unofficial poet laureate of Singapore. "I sing of arms and the man," begins Virgil in his epic poem, "Aeneid" (as translated by AS Kline). "I sing of Singapore", may well be the motto of Thumboo. Words must sing, he said, and while his poems can be intimate and personal, his oeuvre is rich in social commentary. Anti-colonialism, nationalism, multiculturalism have all found expression in his works, adding up to an evocative narrative of Singapore.

He is perhaps best known for his poem, "Ulysses by the Merlion". Published in his eponymous book of poems in 1979, it inspired other poets to write about the Merlion. One couldn't be a true Singapore poet, it was joked, till one had written about the Merlion.

Thumboo has had a profound influence as a pioneer writer and an academic. "Rib of Earth", his first book of poems, was published in 1956 when he was a university student. The University of Singapore was among the earliest to begin studies in Commonwealth literature, at his initiative as an academic. His contributions have been acknowledged both at home and abroad. Besides several Singapore awards, the Cultural Medallion winner also received the inaugural SEA Write Award for Asean writers and the Raja Rao Award for his contributions to the literature of the Indian diaspora.

"For me, the language of poetry has to be taut, has to be intense and has to ring," Thumboo said in an interview with Ronald Klein in 1999. Evening is a perfect example of that — vivid, intense, personal — a poem dedicated to his wife:

The air-con's goblin hum
Shakes the window's furtive light.
Outside, our thunders quarrel.

All is familiar, poised.

The scene described is as vivid and intimate as the bedroom in John Donne's love poems. However, Thumboo could not ignore history being made as Singapore progressed from colonial rule to self-government to full independence. "If you are living in a place like Singapore with so much going on, how can you escape writing about them?" he asked Klein. "I will always write about nation because it is part of my perception," he said in a later interview with Gwee Li Sui.

The Merlion inspired him for two reasons. Influenced by the Irish poet WB Yeats, he believed mythology had an important role in nation building and the mythical "half beast, half-fish" Merlion was a Singapore icon. It represents the people of Singapore in the poem's concluding lines:

This lion of the sea,
This image of themselves.

The poem highlights Singapore's immigrant, multiracial makeup:

Despite unequal ways,
Together they mutate,
Explore the edges of harmony,
Search for a centre;
Have changed their gods,
Kept some memory of their race
In prayer, laughter, the way
Their women dress and greet.

This awareness of Singapore's ethnic and cultural diversity is part of Thumboo's multicultural heritage. Born on November 22, 1933, he had an Indian father and a Chinese mother. His father was a schoolteacher from an Anglicised family, but they lived with his mother's family, who were rich, traditional and Teochew. Living in a big, attap-roofed house on the Mandai foothills, he enjoyed nature, getting wet in the rain, sticking out his tongue to taste the raindrops as a child.

Prof Thumboo reciting a poem at the launch of The Third Map, a collection of his earlier works.

His idyllic childhood shaped him as a poet, but the idyll came to an end with the Japanese Occupation. Uprooted from their home, they moved to Newton and had hard times. They reared pigs, ducks and goats. He had to sell cakes baked by his mother. Later, he worked in a shop. After the war, he went to Victoria School in 1948. That is where he began to write poems. He loved to play with words and began translating Chinese poems with the help of his friends. That inspired him to write his own poems from 1950.

Shamus Frazer, an Oxford-educated English novelist and poet who was teaching at Victoria, became his mentor. He also began mixing in literary circles, meeting teachers, civil servants and others writing in English. "No doubt we were a colony, but we had a distinct middle-class and English-educated way of life," he reminded Klein.

At the same time, he was a nationalist. At the university, he joined the editorial board of *Fajar* (Dawn in Malay), a journal published by the University Socialist Club. In May 1954, *Fajar* published an editorial calling for independence. At that time, Chinese middle school students were clashing with the police over the National Service Ordinance ruling. Thumboo was one of eight university students arrested and tried for sedition. Lee Kuan Yew, who was the club's legal adviser and a *Fajar* subscriber, helped them get acquitted.

"Depart white man," Thumboo wrote in his poem, May 1954, which ends with the lines:

Depart Tom, Dick and Harry,

Gently, with ceremony:

We may still be friends,

Even love you… from a distance.

After graduation, Thumboo worked for the Income Tax Department, the Central Provident Fund Board and briefly at the Singapore Telephone Board before joining the University of Singapore as an assistant lecturer in June 1966. He married his wife Swee Chin in 1963. Thumboo the public poet began to emerge in the second volume, *Gods Can Die*, published in 1977. This was followed by *Ulysses by the Merlion* in 1979.

It contained poems like "Island", about Singapore's transformation from a thriving colony to an industrial powerhouse.

Aminah, Harun now reside in flats,

Go to school while father

Learns a trade.

Along Shipyard Road,

Not far from Bird Park,

A new song in the air:

Cranes and gantries rise;
Dynamo and diesel hum.
Men in overalls and helmets
Wield machines, consulting plans.

While "Island" celebrates the transformation of Singapore, Thumboo is not blind to what money and politics can do to people. He heaps scorn on the jumped-up, ill-bred executive in "Plush":

Proud, uncouth, man,
Is this the tapper's son,
Six years away from Jemaluang
Beneath this slim executive tan?

In Gods Can Die, he takes aim at political opportunists and time-servers:

I have seen powerful men
Undo themselves, keep two realities
One for minor friends, one for the powers that be

Thumboo writes about friendship, politics and change. There is also a love of learning. He has written poems about Victoria School, RELC and the National Library. "Ulysses by the Merlion" is dedicated to Maurice Baker, who taught him at the University of Malaya, and "Fifteen Years After" pays tribute to Shamus Frazer, his earliest mentor. There is also a fascination with words in poems like "Words", "RELC", "Language as Power", "Word as a Linguist", "Words Loop Again" and "Words for the Day". Lyrically, he writes about the interaction between poems and the reader in *The Poetry Reader*:

While by the waters of the Seine more poems gather.
I read them, they read me.

He can use a marvellous economy of words to surprising effect, painting scenes vividly. As in this description of the immigrant experience in his poem "After the Leaving":

There are two countries here:
One securely meets the eye,
The other binds your heart.
This is Perth, and yet Malacca.

He is not happy about what the media and the internet are doing to language. In "Muse in Media", he mourns:

For trade-and-politics are now the hymns.
We lose mysterious richness, marvellous awe
As GATT, MFN… our multiplying acronyms,
Replace redemptive image, metaphor.

"The internet is a double whammy," he complained in the interview with Gwee. "Firstly, it is easy; secondly, its language is such that you don't learn to appreciate beautiful language. And why do you remember poetry? Why do you remember things? Because the language is beautiful. So it's a double loss here."

He has his own explanation for Singapore writers not being as successful as others writing in English. "You see the terrible thing is this: in other parts of the world, the West Indies and so on, the writers' way out of their condition was to write and be successful, to get money," he told Gwee. "Here, most of us are fat cats. You name me one writer who is impoverished. They don't starve: that's my point. There are means; they will always have support."

However, over the years, he has seen how Singapore writing in English, especially the poetry, has developed remarkably. It is sophisticated, inventive, rich, adventurous and as good as any being written in English. The poets are so at home in English that they wield linguistic confidence, can take liberties with it and at the same time create such nuances. Moreover, there is great variety because it draws on our multiculural inheritances.

Thumboo continues to publish. *The Best of Edwin Thumboo*, in 2012, was followed by another anthology, *Word-Gate*, privately published in 2013. Age has leavened his poetry. *Still Travelling* — his last book of new poems published in 2008 when he was 75 — is rich in Biblical themes and memories. However, these are meditations and reflections of a poet who can still be deeply sensuous. The romantic "Evening" is part of *Still Travelling* — and there are other intimate moments like this — the perfectly realised details of a tender touch:

I hear what is not heard: songs of your hair
Against the wind: then forged silence.

I see what is not seen: your fingers climbing

The nape of my neck; swans are in season.
(With the Sixth)

He lives by the pen.

The expectancy sparked by "the fingers climbing" followed by the apparent non sequitur, "swans are in season", makes you pause. You wonder at the mystery of the moment: where will it end, and why the swans? For no reason, you are reminded of Yeats — the romantic Yeats, not the nationalist Yeats — and *The Wild Swans of Coole*:

Unwearied still, lover by lover,

They paddle in the cold

Companionable streams or climb the air;

Their hearts have not grown old;

Passion or conquest, wander where they will,

Attend upon them still.

Poems are what you make of them. As Thumboo himself wrote: "I read them, they read me."

Thumboo's public poetry is eloquent history, but it is his intimate, personal poems that say the things you would tell the one you love if you had a gift for words.

References

Thumboo, Edwin (1979) *May 1954: Ulyssses by the Merlion* p.18
Singapore Heinemann Educational Books (Asia) Ltd
Thumboo, Edwin (1979) *Gods Can Die: Gods Can Die* p.62
Singapore Heinemann Educational Books (Asia) Ltd

BY ABHIJIT NAG

ALL FOR THE BEST

Eugene Wijeysingha not only wrote a history of
Raffles Institution; he made history, too.

H e is a man who recognises the importance of education. Educator and historian Eugene Wijeysingha will be remembered as the headmaster under whom Singapore's famous Raffles Institution became an independent school in 1990. Independence meant that the former government school, founded in 1823, was no longer run by the Ministry of Education but was free to develop its own programmes and resources and — this was controversial — set its own fees. There was an uproar, a flood of letters to the press from the public and Rafflesians alike concerned that bright but poor students would no longer be able to attend Singapore's premier school.

The fees did go up, but there are financial assistance schemes to help those who need them. Wijeysingha himself attended university on a government bursary and tried to help others throughout his career as a teacher. But he also wanted the best for Raffles and there was a price to be paid for that. The school had to "recruit the best teachers from the open market, pay them competitive salaries" in order "to provide the best for the RI boy", he wrote in his book, *For a Better Age: Musings of a Teacher*.

That is the story of Wijeysingha, an idealist who wanted the best for his students, and a realist who accepted that the best cost more.

He was the headmaster of Raffles Institution from 1986 to 1994 when education was going through major changes. "Independent schools were the idea of Dr Tony Tan Keng Yam, who was then the education minister," he says.

Dr Tan wanted more autonomy for schools to encourage innovation. The education system was not likely to improve if the sole initiative came from the ministry, he told *The Straits Times* in 1987. The Anglo-Chinese School and the Chinese High School were the first to go independent in 1988. Independence did not mean privatisation but more autonomy for schools, which would continue to get government funding, said Dr Tan.

Raffles also needed autonomy, thought Wijeysingha when he returned to the school as headmaster in 1986 after an absence of more than 20 years. In his view, a premier institution like Raffles could not be run like any other government school. He proposed the school be managed by an independent board of governors. Government funding for the school should be transferred to the management of the board, he added.

Dr Tan welcomed Wijeysingha's proposals as the best submission he had received in a long time. However, the school did not become independent till 1990. The people had to be persuaded first that Singapore's foremost government school should be made independent. It was so contentious there were debates in Parliament.

The head of Raffles Institution used to be called the "headmaster", but later became the "principal". Wijeysingha restored the old form of address. He preferred to be called "headmaster" like the heads of public schools in Britain. Like them, he expected his students to be "gentlemen", not only good at studies, but also cultured, upright, and good at sports.

He wanted to build, to use his own words, the "rugged Rafflesian". It was not an alien concept. The school had a sporting tradition. But his emphasis on character development and his seminal role in the school invited comparison with a famous English headmaster, Thomas Arnold. The father of the poet Matthew Arnold was the legendary headmaster who brought glory to Rugby School and inspired the book, *Tom Brown's School Days*. Raffles Institution has not inspired such a popular novel, but Wijeysingha has written a history of the school, *The Eagle Breeds a Gryphon*.

Unlike some of the previous headmasters of the school, he was not a Rafflesian but a mission-school boy. Born in 1934 in Negeri Sembilan, Malaysia, he was the third of seven children. Immigrants from Sri Lanka, his father worked for Malayan Railway and his mother was the daughter of an estate overseer. The railway job kept the family on the move until they finally came to Singapore in 1949. That was when Wijeysingha enrolled in St Joseph's Institution.

After school, he wanted to go to university, but his parents could not afford it. So he took a government bursary, which required him to teach for five years upon graduation.

That is how he became a teacher when he graduated from the University of Malaya with a Bachelor of Arts (honours) in history and got his diploma in education. He began his career in 1959 as a teacher at Raffles Institution. He had heard that the late Velauthur Ambiavagar, the school's first Asian principal and a former sportsman, wanted teachers with a sporting background. Wijeysingha enjoyed teaching. He could relate to the young, played games with them and enjoyed their company.

He could also be funny. His wife, Christine, whom he first met at his sister's birthday party when he was 20 and she 17, recalled his way with words. Soon after they met, he wrote to her, asking for her photograph because he would be going to university and needed "inspiration". Instead, she sent him a picture of the Virgin Mary. When they met again, he told her: "I never knew you were the mother of God." They got married in December 1960 when he was 26 and she 23.

Wijeysingha taught at Raffles for seven years. Former prime minister Goh Chok Tong was one of his early students. So were former senior minister of state (foreign affairs) Zainul Abideen Rasheed and former Speaker of Parliament Abdullah Tarmugi. He wanted the very best from his students. "He expected our General Paper essays to be written like research papers," recalled Goh Chok Tong in his foreword to Wijeysingha's book, *For a Better Age: Musings of a Teacher*. "When he returned my first essay, I was stunned," Goh added. "I had scored only 2 out of 10 marks! I looked around and saw shocked faces all around. Most had less than two marks, and a few had half a mark or less. Only Mr Wijeysingha was savouring the moment."

Wijeysingha began writing a history of the school while teaching there. He was the senior history master when Wee Seong Kang, then principal of the school, showed him a bundle of disintegrating, old documents dating back to the beginnings of Raffles Institution. Going through the old letters, Wijeysingha began writing a book, which was first published in 1962. He updated the narrative, covering the years from 1823 to 1985, at the request of former students after he returned to Raffles as headmaster in 1986. *The Eagle Breeds a Gryphon* was further updated in 2004, on request by another group of ex-Rafflesians who wanted a chapter on Raffles Junior College included. "I took the opportunity to update the entire edition, covering my stint as principal and the school's passage to independent status," he says.

He first served as principal of Changkat Changi Secondary School, after teaching at Raffles. He was given the job in 1967, when he was only 33 years old. It was a world removed from Raffles. The students came from poor backgrounds and often missed class to work for money. He wanted to modify the curriculum to suit the abilities of his students, but was told to follow official policy by the Ministry of Education. "I will never forget taking leave of Changkat Changi Secondary School," he later wrote, when the students bade him farewell, showering him with gifts, and the teachers presented him with a Longines watch.

In 1973, he was posted to the Ministry of Education's headquarters. He rose to be deputy director of secondary schools, but he missed the human interaction in schools. "In a school, it's like a family. You are in constant contact with other people," he told *The Straits Times*. "In the ministry, you relate to people through files. I never liked that, the impersonal kind of working relationship." The "impersonal" ministry stint ended when in January 1980 he became principal of Temasek Junior College, a position he held till November 1985.

In 1986, he returned to Raffles as headmaster with momentous consequences for the school. He wanted changes. The school, then located at Grange Road, looked like a "flatted factory," he observed, adding: 'It is pointless for a school to demand and expect high standards of pupils and preach high values when all around they have to contend with an unkempt building."

There were protests. "Most RI boys are proud that the school building was designed by an old RI boy and the then principal, Mr Philip Liau," retorted an Old Boy in a letter to *The Straits Times* on October 29, 1986.

The school moved in mid 1990 to new premises in Bishan, which was originally meant for a junior college.

Wijeysingha in his memoirs mentions how he was influenced by the former Prime Minister Lee Kuan Yew's insistence on efficiency and discipline. He demanded the same high standards at Raffles. Everything had to be immaculate, from the toilets to the lawns, to motivate the students and teachers to do their best. "An environment that reflected high standards all around conditions the outlook of a people," he noted.

He retired as headmaster in 1994, but his legacy endures. Since 2002, the school has been awarding a scholarship in his name to honour his contributions. The $1,000 annual scholarship goes to the Secondary 4 student who best embodies the Rafflesian spirit.

Wijeysingha tempered discipline with understanding, listening to his students' problems and trying to help them. He had known what it was like to go hungry during the Japanese Occupation. Later, to get through university, he taught English to police constables at night. When as a young teacher at Raffles he saw some students unable to pay their Cambridge Examination fees, he was immediately moved to act. He appealed to his fellow teachers to contribute one dollar a month to a teachers' fund to help pupils in need. Some gave grudgingly and tried to humiliate him. "The handful who did not agree to the proposal would take out a couple of coins, roll them along the wooden floor of the staff common room, and then watch me scurry around to locate them under tables and chairs," he wrote in his memoirs. But, he added, "I did not mind."

He was inspired by his faith to help others. A Catholic and a mission-school boy, he drew inspiration from two French missionaries, one of whom spent time with leprosy patients at Trafalgar Home while the other bequeathed his inheritance to the poor. "That to me was service to others. That to me was what Catholicism was all about," he wrote

He admired other selfless church workers he met. A group of volunteers from the Church of St Vincent de Paul made a profound impression on him. He met them in the 1970s. Once

The former student who once sat in class, graduated to become 'headmaster' in RI.

they visited a man suffering from tuberculosis. Cheerfully, the man welcomed them into his house and offered them coffee from a flask. "I hesitated, but the others drank it without a second thought. So I was forced to follow their example," he recalled.

On another occasion, they took a poor old man in his car to a hospital. They had to walk up a steep slope after parking the car. After a few steps, the old man sat down to rest. A curious passer-by asked one of the volunteers if the old man was his father. "He nodded his head to say, 'Yes'," recalled Wijeysingha. He can't forget the sympathy and respect shown by the church worker, who wasn't ashamed to call the poor old man his father.

Wijeysingha has written a church history, *Going Forth: The Catholic Church in Singapore, 1819 – 2004*. "In the course of working on it and as the story unfolded, I experienced a sense of personal enrichment," he wrote in the preface to the book, published in 2006.

Wijeysingha still feels passionately about Raffles Institution, which he left more than 20 years ago. He wrote to the chairman of the RI board of governors when he read an article in *The Straits Times* making reference to fewer boys from the lower income group opting for RI and that RI was offering scholarships to primary school pupils from poor backgrounds, ostensibly as an incentive to opt for RI. Boys should not be induced to attend Raffles, he said, the school's reputation should be enough to attract students. They should be eligible for financial assistance after — not before — they join the school, he added.

He lives in quiet retirement with his wife. His elder daughter, his second child, is a senior teacher in the primary section of the Convent of the Holy Infant Jesus in Toa Payoh. His second son, Vincent Wijeysingha, who has a doctorate in social policy from Sheffield University and worked for 10 years in the UK, is leaving Singapore again for an overseas job after a stint in politics. Wijeysingha's younger daughter, who graduated from Murdoch University in Australia, lives with her family in the United States. His youngest son died of an asthma attack during a holiday overseas at the age of 22. His eldest son, who suffered from epilepsy and lived with him, died in 2015.

He spends his days reading, surfing the internet, solving Sudoku puzzles and assembling plastic models of famous naval vessels. The model ships reflect his love for history. The ships in his collection include scale models of famous warships such as the *USS New York* and the *USS Kidd*. He reads books on various subjects, but mainly on politics. Recently he read *That Used to be Us* by the New York Times columnist Thomas Friedman and Michael Mandelbaum. The subtitle of the book, *How America Fell behind in the World It Invented and How We Can Come Back*, reflects his own interest in history and progress. That was why he sought changes at Raffles, to make Singapore's premier school even better.

Significantly, he doesn't mention writing among his pastimes. It seems a curious omission for a prolific writer with a dozen books to his credit. He also used to write newspaper columns about his personal experiences and offering advice to students. But, no, he hasn't written anything of late. "I stopped in 2014 after 12 books," he said. "All my writings were at the request of others," he added. "People approached me to write." He wrote the history of Raffles Institution when asked by the former principal, Wee Seong Kang. The book about the Catholic Church was at the request of the Archbishop, His Most Rev. Nicholas Chia. The newspaper columns were requested by editors.

Maybe he will pick up the pen again, or peck away at the keyboard, when asked to write. Anyone who has read his books can be sure that that, too, will be eminently readable.

By ABHIJIT NAG

FEATS OF GLORY

Former sprint queen Glory Barnabas hasn't left
the field yet. At 70, she is still a winner.

Age hasn't caught up with Glory Barnabas. Lithe and lean, the former sprint queen still runs and jumps, as she always has. A woman like her who ran in the SEA Games even when she was three months' pregnant can't be expected to just hang up her running shoes. The difference is, she won her latest medals for high jump and long jump. That's unusual for a girl renowned for her 200-metre dash, but she's not your run-of-the-mill sprinter. She is Singapore's Glory.

At 71 years old, she takes the bus from her home in Marine Parade to Springfield Secondary School in Tampines, where she teaches physical education (PE), character and Citizenship Education (CCE) Almost half a century has elapsed since her glory days when she sprinted to gold, silver and bronze for Singapore in the late 1960s and early 1970s. You are only young once. But life goes on — and the former track star is taking it in her stride, though not with the élan of youth but with the gamely knowledge of the wise.

Glory has always been game, from childhood. She loved to run with other children and dug a sandpit for long jumps outside her house.

Her latest medals — gold in the high jump and silver in the long jump in the women's 70–74 age group at the 2014, International Gold Masters in Kyoto, Japan — were no accidents. She practised jumps even when she was a sprinter.

"It was part of the training," she said, sitting in her living room, stroking Romeo, her 14-year-old Pomeranian with cataract in one eye. She and her husband, Edwin Barnabas, bought the apartment, in an estate for civil servants, back in the 1970s. They got married in 1966, just one year after independence, and live with their daughter, Jennifer, a tutor.

Edwin, a former teacher, was an athlete in his schooldays in Raffles Institution. But, when his wife talks about how hard she trained, he interjected, "I thought she was mad!" They both laughed.

She loved playing netball when she was a student at Paya Lebar Methodist Girls' School. Playing the centre position, she could run almost the entire court. She had plenty of encouragement. There were no PE teachers then, but her teachers did the best they could, buying her nourishing eggs and food because her mother said she was anaemic. Lacking proper training facilities at school, she and her friends used the grass track at the former Mayfair Primary School. She was sent for competitions where beating rival — richer — schools like Raffles Girls' Secondary was a thrill.

Glory was training to be a teacher when she got into the national team. It happened by chance. She was in her second year at the Teachers' Training College (now the National Institute of Education) in 1962 when she came in first at a university meet although she was a substitute with no athletic training. The late Tan Eng Yoon, a lecturer at the college, was so impressed he said: "You must come for training." "That's how I got into the nationals," she recalled.

As a trainee teacher, she taught in the morning, attended classes at the Teachers' Training College in Paterson Road in the afternoon, and trained as an athlete in the evening at Farrer Park. Running on the bitumen track felt like running in a car park, she says. But a champion was in the making.

She won her first Southeast Asian Peninsular (SEAP) Games medals in Bangkok in 1967 when she took the bronze in both 100 metres and 200 metres. She collected the silver in both the events in the 1969 SEAP Games in Rangoon. Finally, she struck gold in the 1973 SEAP Games in Singapore.

Glory who started competing in the Masters in 1981, won Gold in long jump, at the 5th. Asian Masters Championships, in Tainan City, Taiwan.

She won the 200 metres, which was the most memorable race in her life. Speeding into second place near the halfway mark, she put on a final burst of speed in the last 100 metres, pipping the Burmese frontrunner, Than Than, in a photo finish. She also won the 4x100-metre relay with her team mates, Heather Marican, Gan Bee Wah and Sheila Fernando. She was three months' pregnant when she ran in the 1975 SEAP Games in Bangkok. Her brother died in a car crash during the Games and she returned home, pulling out of the competition. But the relay team was short of runners, so she went back to take part in the relay, but they did not win any medals.

Glory also won a silver in the 1970 Bangkok Asian Games and silver and bronze in the 1974 Tehran Games. She can't forget the 4x400-metre relay in Tehran which the Singaporeans lost to the Japanese. She ran the first leg and passed the baton to Lee Tai Jong. But Lee was a "half-miler", not a sprinter, and she lost ground. Maimoon Azlan narrowed the gap in the third leg and Chee Swee Lee, the last runner, almost caught up with the Japanese. The Singaporeans finished second and took the silver, not the gold, but set a new national record. They completed 4x400 metres in 3 minutes and 43.8 seconds, a record yet to be broken.

Glory retired from the national team in her early 30s in 1977 but returned to compete in masters' meets from 1981. She treasures the 200 metres' gold she won in the World Masters in Melbourne in 1987. Even people in their 70s and 80s turn up for the events, she said, accompanied by their families who cheer them on. Singapore will get to see them when the Asian Masters is held here in 2016. Glory twinkles with anticipation. She is president of the Singapore Masters Athletics, an association for masters athletes, which will be involved in the event.

To succeed, athletes need "CPF", one of her coaches said, by which he meant "commitment, passion and focus". Glory must have loads of "CPF". The former champion who asserted, "I ran for passion, not money," is still running and teaching. She has a passion for both. As she once quipped, "I aspire to inspire before I expire!"

Glory chose teaching because she loves children and the joy that teaching brings. A teacher since 1964, she taught at Charlton Primary and Mountbatten Primary before going to Chelsea College of Physical Education in Britain on a British Council scholarship. She returned in 1972 to teach at Willow Avenue Secondary. In 1986, she set up and headed the PE department at Tampines Junior College. She retired but returned as an adjunct teacher in Springfield.

Emily Huang, the national triathlete, was inspired by her to become a PE teacher. Emily, now head of the department of PE at Yishun Town Secondary School, was her student at Tampines Junior College in 1994-95. She said: "It was not really the place that I had wanted to go to. However, after receiving my O-Level results, I chose to stay on because of Mrs Glory Barnabas.

"Back then, Mrs Barnabas was the HOD of PE and the teacher-in-charge of track and field. She was around to train me even though I was a middle-distance runner and not a sprinter like her. Even when Mrs Barnabas was not around, she would make sure that there was always a teacher coach to train me. "I had some discipline issues as a student. I had some difficulty reaching school on time. One day, I decided to be early for once, and I reached school at 7am! As I walked through the school gate and past the school track, I noticed a lady training diligently at the track. I stopped to watch as I was quite impressed with the drills she was performing. Initially I thought that lady was someone from the public, because I know the school opens the track to the public at certain times of the day, but to my surprise, that lady was Mrs Barnabas! I knew that Mrs Barnabas was a former national athlete, but that to me was her past, until I saw her in action that morning! That role-modelling, sheer discipline and commitment in her training inspired and impressed me so much that I knew I wanted to teach PE, and be just like her!"

Education Minister Heng Swee Keat, in a speech at the Ministry of Education Staff Workplan Seminar held in 2014, mentioned Glory and Emily to show how succeeding generations of teachers influence one another. Glory, he recalled, was inspired to teach by Claudette Poulier, her teacher at Paya Lebar Methodist Girls. She, in turn, inspired Emily, who motivated her student, the cyclist Dinah Chan, to be a PE teacher.

It's amazing when you think Glory has been teaching longer than Singapore has been a nation. Amazing — till you remember her teacher, Mrs Poulier, retired only recently after 63 years as an educator. One must marvel at their spirit and dedication. Smiling, joking, excited about the Asian Masters to be held in Singapore, Glory doesn't appear in the least bit tired of school or sports. The former sprint queen is a marathoner in life. An interviewer once asked her what kept her going. Back came the reply: "I run for my Lord."

BY ABHIJIT NAG

GAME FOR LIFE

He was the first Asian to be a World Cup referee,
but football was not the only love of George Suppiah.

S unlight streamed through the open front door and windows into the eighth-storey, corner HDB apartment, catching the pictures in the hall. One showed her with her cousin, the former President, SR Nathan; in another, her husband stood alone with a football in his hand, the Fifa referee's badge on his chest. Govindasamy Suppiah — better known as George Suppiah — shot to fame as the first Asian to be appointed a World Cup referee. It did not come easy, but neither did marrying the woman he loves.

Sitting on a sofa in a sari, looking much younger than her 85 years, Madam Vallambal cracked a smile as she recalled they were teenagers in love. "We had to wait a long time to get married," she said with a twinkle in her eye.

It was the same story when it came to the World Cup.

Suppiah, who passed away in December 2012, was amazed when he was called up for the tournament in West Germany in 1974. "I thought I might have a chance in 1970. I knew I was earmarked and made it to the final 50. But in the end, they only chose 33 and I was knocked out. After that, I didn't bother keeping track anymore," he told the Asian Football Confederation.

He did not even know he had been selected until he got the news from his boss, Joe David, in the physical education section of the Ministry of Education. "I had no idea. Apparently, it was on the news wires and the sports editor of the local newspaper had called up Joe and told him about my appointment," he said. "It was very heart-warming."

He officiated at the Poland-Haiti match in which the Poles won 7-0. His daughter, Shamini, recalled, "As the first Asian to officiate at the World Cup, he had to work extra hard to prove his calibre. He was probably the tiniest referee there (1.6m) but he exerted his authority on the game through his confidence and dignity."

Godfrey Robert, former sports editor of *The Straits Times*, wrote, "Even before he stepped onto the Munich pitch, there were minor protests by both teams about handing their game over to a referee from an 'unknown' country. Suppiah was not upset with this remark, and he showed his supreme talent by handling the match with distinction, earning eight out of 10 marks, one above the average." Suppiah told Robert: "In the end, the managers and coaches of both teams came up to me and congratulated me."

He went on to be a linesman at the Brazil-Holland World Cup semi-final match in Dortmund. It was, as he said, a memorable experience: "There were so many stars on either side, and many came up to me to intimidate me, but I was never cowed. I applied the rules correctly." He was the only Singaporean to referee at the World Cup until Shamsul Maidin was called up for the tournament in 2006, also held in Germany.

Born in 1929, Suppiah served as a referee for 25 years, from 1953 to 1978, including in the Asian Games and the Olympics. But not everyone was happy. "As a child, I didn't love the game," said Shamini. "It took my dad away from me much of the time." Suppiah, who became a FIFA referee in 1966, travelled around the world, conducting courses, training referees. His wife, who accompanied him to the World Cup in West Germany, came to love the game, like the man himself.

They met for the first time at a sports meet. He was then a student at Raffles Institution, she at Raffles Girls'. They lived near each other in Little India — he in Owen Road, she in Rangoon Road. He used to come to her house to give private tuition to one of her nephews. But their families did not know that they had fallen in love.

Suppiah, whose father worked at the Raffles Hotel, came from a conservative family. Once he became a school teacher, his mother took him to India to arrange his marriage, but he rejected every girl he saw. Finally, she asked him if there was anyone he loved and that was when he told her about his sweetheart.

It came as a shock. "His relatives did not come for our wedding," recalled Madam Vallambal. "They opposed our marriage because we were of a different caste." But it was a "grand wedding", she added, attended by all her relatives and his numerous friends.

She giggled as she recalled how her life changed completely once she got married in 1957. "I had learnt shorthand and typing along with baking and embroidery after completing school." But the Suppiahs had no use for her typing or shorthand. They lived in a shophouse packed with relatives Suppiah's father had brought over from his village in India but whose lifestyles had not changed. They spoke in Tamil and the women ate after the men.

After rejecting every marriage proposal George Suppiah blew the whistle about his secret love — a love that still lives within Mdm Vallambal's heart.

They were a joint family and expected to stay together. "Don't take away our son," Suppiah's mother told Madam Vallambal.

Suppiah was too close to his family and happy in Little India to go anywhere else. He continued to live with his elder brother in the Owen Road shophouse, even after he bought an apartment in Neptune Court on the East Coast.

But, like his wife, he underwent a change, too. He went to Loughborough University in England after marriage for training as a physical education teacher. "That was where he began to be called "George" because people found it hard to pronounce his name, "Govindasamy", recalled his daughter.

PN Sivaji, former Singapore national coach, recalled, "George Suppiah, whom close friends called "Sup", oozed class. He refereed matches in which I played. I have watched him deal with some very difficult players and learnt from his man-management methods. I used to admire the polished manner he spoke and the way he managed difficult situations. He has never shouted at anyone, but he always knew how to get his point across. "Apart from having been an excellent referee, he also coached the national youth soccer team and the Combined Schools team in the '60s."

A gifted athlete who played football, hockey, cricket, tennis and bowls, Suppiah had green thumbs and loved animals. There were always pets about the house. He didn't give up sports even in his old age. Suppiah, who retired as head of the physical education department of the Anglo-Chinese Junior College, continued to train youngsters at Farrer Park and the Singapore Indian Association.

Ever resilient, he continued to go about, driving a sporty blue MG, even after losing two of his toes to diabetes. However life could not go on forever. In May 2012, after watching the doctors' annual football friendly match from the sidelines instead of the centrefield as the referee, he had to be admitted to hospital. There would be no comebacks. After seven long months, he died in Tan Tock Seng Hospital on December 7, 2012. He was 83.

The wake continued for two days, with complete strangers pouring in to share their sorrow. Shamini recalled a little girl sobbing uncontrollably. "I hadn't seen her before, but found she was one of the kids he had been training. She had been out of the country and had just landed at the airport when she saw the news on television. Straight away, she wanted her mother to bring her to the wake."

"Children loved Dad," she added. "He made sure they have the boots and equipment to play sports if they could not afford them. He used to say there was a time when he had no money, too, and had to walk to school."

His contributions did not go unrecognised. He was among the earliest nominees for the Senior Citizens Awards, said his daughter. He received a Distinguished Service Award and a Gold Award from the Asian Football Confederation in 2009 – and the Lifetime Achievement Award from the Malaysian Indian Congress (MIC) Youth Wing two weeks before he died.

The man is gone, but not the warmth and hospitality he loved. Friends drop by at all hours at the apartment where he lived in his old age with his wife and daughter and her husband. Madam Vallambal still cooks a sumptuous spread on Sundays. And, yes, they are still living in Little India.

BY ABHIJIT NAG

PIONEER DOCTOR

Dr James Supramaniam, aka "Dr Tan Tock Seng",
helped eradicate what was Singapore's No 1
killer disease in the 1950s and early 60s.

D r James MJ Supramaniam went for a walk every day after he retired. He would go out wearing a tweed deerstalker hat like Sherlock Holmes, recalled his daughter-in-law, Datin Margy Supramaniam. His likeness to the legendary detective did not end there. He had been an investigator, too, leading a Singapore-UK joint research project probing the link between smoking and lung cancer. In fact, Dr Supramaniam was ahead of his time. He wanted smoking banned in public places more than 50 years ago when smokers puffed freely everywhere.

He had the acumen to see smoking could be bad for you – even if you did not smoke — long before most of the world had woken up to the dangers of passive smoking and secondary smoke. His warning against public smoking went unheeded, but he won his other battle — against tuberculosis or TB, Singapore's no 1 killer in the 1950s and early 60s.

When Dr Supramaniam died in 2008 at the ripe old age of 87, tributes poured in, recalling his leading role in the battle to rid Singapore of TB. He fought to save others after losing his parents early — and his elder brother in World War II.

Born in Malaya in 1921, he lost his mother when he was only two years old.

His father, the Rev James Arumugam Supramaniam, came from a staunch Hindu aristocratic Jaffna family but converted to Christianity in 1894 while studying at Anglo-Chinese School (ACS). Rev Supramaniam co-founded the Ceylon Tamils' Association in Singapore in 1910 and was headmaster at both ACS Seremban and ACS Penang, and the Methodist District Superintendent for Selangor, Negri Sembilan and Pahang.

Like his father, Dr Supramaniam attended ACS in Singapore before the family moved to Kuala Lumpur. As a boy, he used to accompany his father on visits to parishioners in villages in Pahang and Negri Sembilan. They travelled in a Baby Austin. The boy had to wind up the crank shaft to keep the car going and hold up bright lights and bang sticks to scare off animals.

But Rev Supramaniam did not live to see his son grow up. The boy was only 15 when he became an orphan. He was then raised by his eldest sister, Rose, a concert pianist and soprano.

Clever and hardworking, he passed the Senior Cambridge with flying colours as the top student at Methodist Boys' School in Kuala Lumpur. He entered the King Edward VII College of Medicine in Singapore on a colonial scholarship.

His studies were interrupted by World War II. He joined the British Medical Auxiliary Service in December 1941 after the attack on Pearl Harbour — and was wounded when the Japanese invaded Singapore. He was hit in the leg by a Japanese shell while burying a colleague killed the day before.

Other medical students in the burial party were killed in the shelling. The war also claimed the life of his elder brother, George. A gifted surgeon, he died while helping British prisoners-of-war in Kuching during the Japanese Occupation.

After the British surrendered, Dr Supramaniam risked certain death by smuggling medicine and supplies to other war casualties in Woodbridge Hospital under the noses of the Japanese guards. For this, he received a medal from King George VI at the end of the war.

Dr Supramaniam, who had to work in a bacteriology unit at the Singapore General Hospital (SGH) under the Japanese Occupation, resumed his medical studies after the war, graduating in 1951.

Although the shrapnel from his wartime injury had left a hole in his leg, he rebuilt his muscles through strenuous exercise and weight training and excelled in sports. He was a fine footballer, a tennis and badminton ace, and a champion athlete.

He was also vice-president of the University of Malaya Students' Union, national chairman of the Singapore Students' Christian Movement and a violinist in the university orchestra.

In 1955, he went to Ceylon to marry Eunice Princess Jebaranee Aiyathurai (Ranee), who had spent part of her childhood in Malaya, where her father, Dr Aiyathurai, had been physician to Sultan Ibrahim and the first non-white chief medical officer of the Southern Malayan states.

Soon after his wedding, Dr Supramaniam was sent by the colonial authorities to Britain as part of the Malayanisation programme to train Singaporeans to take over the running of Singapore. He trained at the universities of Edinburgh, Glasgow and Wales as a cardio-thoracic specialist and returned to Singapore in 1958. He was appointed chest physician at

From left, Dr Supramaniam, Dr Eddie Ho and Singapore's second President, Benjamin Sheares. Dr Ho, who was Permanent Secretary, Social Affairs, later served as Ambassador to Russia and High Commissioner in London where he died in office.

Tan Tock Seng Hospital, treating TB, asthma, chest infections and lung cancer. "Doctor Tan Tock Seng" became his nickname. In 1967, he was appointed medical superintendent of Tan Tock Seng Hospital. He helped transform it from a TB hospital to a leading general hospital with more beds than SGH.

In the mid 1960s, he became the first Singaporean chairman of the Civil Medical Aviation Board. There he set up the framework for certification of Singapore and Malaysian pilots, both civil and military.

Dr Supramaniam chaired numerous government committees and boards, including the Medical/Clinical Research Committee of Singapore, and had over 26 publications to his name dating from 1958. He broke new ground with his treatment of tuberculosis with the drug Cycloserine, collaborating with one of the leading authorities in the field, Dr RJ Grove-White.

From 1971 to 1981, he was the deputy permanent secretary of health. He retired in 1981 due to ill health.

He helped many people, including Tamil doctors who fled from Jaffna during the fighting in Sri Lanka. He gave them jobs and helped them "establish themselves" in Singapore, wrote his daughter-in-law, Margy, in a loving tribute to him.

He had a happy marriage. His wife, who trained as a botanist at the University of Ceylon, gave up her job as a teacher to give full support to her husband and their three children.

Dr Supramaniam always made time for his family, said his son, Dato Paul Supramaniam, a prominent international lawyer. When the doctor discovered his son was "keen on the piano", he made it a point to be home at a certain time so they could listen to classical music together. Dr Supramaniam also loved literature. To inspire his son to work hard as a boy, he quoted the poet, Longfellow: "The heights by great men reached and kept, were not obtained by sudden flight. But they, while their companions slept, were toiling upward in the night."

He hoped his son would follow in his footsteps.

"But when he found out that I do not have the aptitude for science, let alone medicine, he did not show his disappointment. Instead, he was very encouraging and would go through my law papers with me whenever he had the time," said Paul.

When Dr Supramaniam died, Minister Vivian Balakrishnan wrote to Paul: "Your father made a huge impact on many lives, both in his personal and professional life. He belonged to the founding generation of Singapore who laboured under difficult and challenging conditions to make life so much better for us and our children."

More than a thousand people attended Dr Supramaniam's funeral wake. One of Paul's army colleagues, a colonel, who did not know Dr Supramaniam personally, insisted on joining the funeral procession. "Your father's anti-TB efforts saved my dad and gave affordable screening measures for my brothers, sister and me," he told Paul.

A devout Christian, Dr Supramaniam served the Methodist Church, notably as Lay Leader of the Tamil Conference of the Methodist Church of Singapore. He sang his favourite hymns with joy even when his health was failing.

He had a strong sense of mission. This is clear from the words with which he concluded an article on thoracic medicine, which appeared in the *Annals of the Academy of Medicine (NS)* in October 1973. He ended the article with a quote from "the great physician Sir William Osler":

"The practice of medicine is an art, not a trade; a calling, not a business; a calling in which your heart will be exercised equally with your head. To prevent disease, to relieve suffering and to heal the sick, this is our work."

This sense of calling took him as Singapore's representative to the World Health Assembly. He also helped, as a World Health Organisation Fellow, to establish medical services in countries such as Kenya and Taiwan as part of Singapore's soft-power diplomacy in the early and mid 1960s.

He received the Public Administration Gold Medal from the then President, Benjamin Sheares, in 1974. The citation read: "It is not many men who choose to tread the hard and difficult path of service to the community when easier and often more lucrative opportunities are open to them. Dr James Supramaniam is of this breed."

BY SHEILA OLIVEIRO

GOING THE DISTANCE

Long-distance running queen K Jayamani is the only woman in Singapore to win the gold in marathon — and it was not even her favourite event.

More than 30 years ago, a girl next door with few supporters stepped gingerly onto the running tracks with little hope of making it to the finishing line. Not only did K Jayamani, 28, surprise herself by completing the marathon at the 1983 Southeast Asia (SEA) Games — she won a gold medal for Singapore. To crown it all, she remains to this day the nation's only female marathon gold medallist.

Now 59, Singapore's long-distance running queen recalls the struggle at the time when athletes were given little recognition and encouragement. A gardener's daughter who worked as an administrative clerk, she did not get leave with pay to compete in track events. She had to use up her annual leave and, when that was exhausted, she had to resort to taking unpaid leave.

"This is the first time the marathon was introduced in the SEA Games and I was asked to run. I had only two trial runs before the marathon," she said.

The Games were held in Singapore and Jaya was expected to win in her pet events, the 1,500metres and 3,000metres. She bagged the bronze in the 3000m event but none in the 1,500m. After that, she had to pin all her hopes on the marathon.

On the morning of the race, Jaya woke up early at 4 am, not in the best physical or mental condition. She was going through her woman's cycle, which was not easy to deal with, especially with a long marathon ahead. She also had to face two strong and experienced opponents — Thailand's Lohachart Yupin, who ran the London and Thai marathons and was the favourite to win, and Mar Mar Min, a well-known Burmese runner.

As expected, when the race started, Mar Mar Min was leading the pack for the first 21 km and Jaya was trailing, bunched with the second group of runners.

Jaya who ran a lonely race, enters an empty stadium, alone.

Jaya sharing her victory with Mar Mar Min and Lohachart Yupin, 1st and 2nd runners-up. According to Jaya, "there are no losers in sports."

"The roads were deserted with no one to cheer you on except for volunteers stationed at intermittent water points and sponging stations who encouraged you. The route took me from the National Stadium, Mountbatten, Fort Road and the East Coast to Changi Village, where we turned and headed to the East Coast and entered Fort Road, Mountbatten Road, Stadium Road, passed the Indoor Stadium and headed to Stadium Walk leading into the National Stadium."

"At this point, I could not see the lead runners. I could only make out a faint mix of red and orange flashing lights coming from police and route marshal cars."

"It was a lonely run along East Coast Road, which is a long stretch. At the 30 km mark, I began to pursue the frontrunners and started closing in. I was now in third position, behind Thailand's Yupin. As I overtook her, I was taken aback when I heard a voice say in Tamil, "*avel shagapooral, nee poh*" (she is drained, you go). That message really spurred me on for I knew he was referring to Mar Min. When I reached the 35 km mark, I started seeing Mar's silhouette and, as I got closer, I could see that she was almost walking. I told myself that I had to push myself. So I began increasing my pace. I also made up my mind to overtake Mar. Just as I was set to go, I noticed that the escort car had stopped at the junction of East Coast Road and Fort Road. I knew that it is customary for the vehicle to halt when the first runner stops. I realised then that there was no hope for Mar and that I had to seize this opportunity to win a medal for my country. I was really exhausted but told myself to push on. I put a lot of mental and physical pressure on myself — qualities I inherited from my late father. This was also my only chance to win gold for Singapore."

"As I pounded the road, I saw that Mar had stopped running just before Fort Road. Although it is every runner's desire to win a competition, it is also very painful to see an athlete of her standing in such a situation. As I passed her, I said, 'Ma, come let's run together.' I could tell from her look that she shared the same dream to win the gold. We had competed in three SEA Games and had become close friends."

"I passed Mar and I was inspired by a few bystanders, local athletes and Mobile Squad officers, cheering 'Go, girl, go'."

And go Jaya did, puffing and gasping for breath to complete the race of her life and bring glory to her country.

K Jayamani's records still stand unbroken to this day: 1,500m in 4 minutes and 31 seconds in Germany in 1982 — and 3,000m in 9 minutes and 51 seconds, also in Germany the same year.

BY ABHIJIT NAG

LABOUR LEADER

The postal workers' strike for better pay in 1952 helped trade unionist G Kandasamy find his calling and also their lawyer, Lee Kuan Yew, make his name as a leader.

P ostal workers helped Singapore become Singapore by putting their faith in a young lawyer. Later, in his old age, Lee Kuan Yew wrote about how he became a leader after the 1952 postal workers' agitation when Singapore was still under British rule. Not that he was their first choice. In fact, the young lawyer, just returned from Cambridge, looked distinctly inexperienced for such a role.

But Govindasamy Kandasamy, better known as G Kandasamy, desperately needed a lawyer to negotiate with the authorities for better pay and conditions. His Singapore Union of Postal and Telecommunications Workers and the Postal and Telecommunications Uniformed Staff Union had suddenly lost their legal adviser. John Eber, their Cambridge-educated Eurasian lawyer, had been arrested in an anti-communist crackdown. Kandasamy wanted his friend, the veteran lawyer Michael Laycock, to represent the workers. However, Laycock said he was busy. Instead, he recommended his junior, Lee.

"I accepted because I trusted Laycock's judgment," Kandasamy said later. The story is told in Peter Lim's biography of the union leader, *That Fellow Kanda*.

Lee took up the case with the authorities. After three months of negotiations, with no settlement in sight, the postal workers went on strike on May 13, 1952. Mail piled up. Though inconvenienced, people sympathised with the underpaid workers. The Malay and Chinese papers supported the strikers. So did Lee's friend, S Rajaratnam, who lambasted the authorities in the *Singapore Standard*. The government gave in. Negotiations resumed on May 26 and ended with a "satisfactory agreement", recalled Lee.

It was a great victory for him. He gained recognition and credibility, as he acknowledged in his autobiography, *The Singapore Story: The Memoirs of Lee Kuan Yew*. "I was no longer just a brash young lawyer back from Cambridge with academic honours. I had led striking workers, spoken up for them and was trusted by them... I gained enormously in the estimation of thousands of workers in Singapore and Malaya without frightening the English-educated intelligentsia. My friends and I were now convinced that in the unions we would find the mass base and, by extension, the political muscle we had been seeking..."

Kandasamy's star rose with Lee's. The union leader was drawn into the Oxley Road Circle, which met at Lee's home to discuss issues and strategies. In 1953, he went to Oxford on a UNESCO fellowship for a nine-month course in industrial relations at Ruskin College. From there, he went to Uppsala, Sweden, for another course in worker education and industrial relations on his Unesco fellowship. Then he visited Germany, Belgium, France, the International Labour Organisation in Geneva with his fellow scholars — and went to Israel on his own to see the new nation.

Lee was busy, too. After forming the People's Action Party in 1954, he stood for election for the first time in 1955. He was elected to the Legislative Assembly, which replaced the old Legislative Council, from Tanjong Pagar. Unionists helped him rally working-class voters. Kandasamy also played a bigger role, becoming the secretary-general of the Singapore Trades Union Congress in 1957. He was elected to the Assembly as the PAP member for Kampong Kapor in the 1959 general election, when Singapore achieved self-government, and became the Deputy Speaker of the House.

It was a phenomenal success for a union leader who had sold cakes on the streets of Butterworth as a boy and newspapers as a young man in Singapore.

Born on May 23, 1921, in Province Wellesley, Kandasamy was two years older than Lee. His father, Govindasamy, was a government employee who also dealt in property and owned several houses. He lost his fortune, however, in the Great Depression like Lee's grandfather did and died when Kandasamy was only 11 years old, leaving him with his mother and younger brother. To make ends meet, his mother made Nonya and Indian cakes, which the boy sold on the streets after school. He attended St Mark's School in Butterworth and, later, Penang Anglo-Chinese School.

His mother remarried. His stepfather, Sathiappan, was a telecommunications official. The family moved to Penang and later came to Singapore. They lived in government quarters in May Road, near Buffalo Road, in Little India.

Kandasamy went to St Joseph's Institution. After passing the Senior Cambridge examination in 1936, he wanted to study agriculture at a college in Serdung, north of the Causeway. His family could not afford the fees. So he sought a letter from the school principal that would help him get the college hostel fees waived. However, as the school's policy was to help Roman Catholics only, he was unable to go to the college of his choice.

Kandasamy began looking for a job. In 1937, he started work as a postal clerk at the General Post Office in Fullerton Building. The official who hired him persuaded him to join the Singapore Volunteer Force. That was where he met Goh Keng Swee, who later became Finance Minister and then Deputy Prime Minister. When the Japanese invaded Singapore, Kandasamy served as a signaller, transmitting military orders in Morse code.

During the Japanese Occupation, Kandasamy became a newsvendor, selling the Japanese *Syonan Shimbun* (Singapore Daily News). He picked up the language from the newspaper and went back to work at the GPO. Pleased with his initiative, his Japanese boss sent him to a language class and used him as an interpreter. He was transferred to Kuala Lumpur when the Japanese moved the postal headquarters there.

When the Japanese surrendered in August 1945, Kandasamy was told he could return to Singapore. He resumed working at the GPO.

Soon he became involved in union activities, which started after the war. The Trade Union Ordinance, enacted in 1940 when the Labour Party joined Winston Churchill's wartime coalition government, finally came into operation in 1946, allowing workers to form unions in Singapore. Kandasamy and his colleagues founded the Singapore Union of Postal and Telecommunications Workers in December 1946 and it was duly registered it in March 1947. The successful 1952 postal workers' strike transformed the political landscape in Singapore. Lee, who was elected to the Assembly in 1955, led the PAP to a sweeping election victory and became the first Prime Minister of Singapore in 1959. Kandasamy, who won the seat of Kampong Kapor in Little India, was elected Deputy Speaker of the Assembly.

His rise did not go unchallenged. He should resign as secretary-general of the Singapore National Trades Union Congress (SNTUC) because he was now a member of the ruling party and therefore could not represent the workers, contended an anonymous letter writer in *The Straits Times* who claimed to be a union secretary.

Kandasamy did not step down. Instead, he became the leader of another union he helped launch. The Amalgamated Union of Public Employees was formed in 1959 after civil servants felt the pinch of pay cuts. After coming to power, Lee declared the treasury was almost bare, depleted by the previous government, and told government employees to tighten their belts. The Singapore Federation of Unions of Government Employees protested and submitted proposals, which were rejected by the government.

Moderate unionists, including those close to the PAP, realised the pay cuts were inevitable, given the state of the finances, and tried to find a solution. That was how the AUPE came into being. It was formed on September 26, 1959, with the merger of the Singapore Union of Postal and Telecommunications Workers and the Postal and Telecommunications Uniformed

Photos courtesy of Amalgamated Union of Public Employees

AUPE Executive Council Meeting at its HQ in Serangoon Road.

Staff Union, the two most active public sector unions. SR Nathan, who later became the President of Singapore, joined the new union as a vice-president while Kandasamy was the general secretary. Seven more unions came into the fold. The new union showed its métier when in 1961, it successfully negotiated a partial reinstatement of the allowances that had been cut.

Kandasamy also changed jobs in 1961. He resigned as Deputy Speaker and became Parliamentary Secretary to the Ministry of Culture. Again, there were misgivings. The staff side of the Singapore Civil Service Joint Council expressed concern over the union leader's appointment as a Parliamentary Secretary.

Kandasamy, nevertheless, continued his union activities — and cleared the way for the formation of the National Trades Union Congress. The Singapore Trades Union Congress, for which he had served as secretary-general, split up when leftists expelled from the PAP formed the Barisan Sosialis in July 1961. The leftists formed their own Singapore Association of Trade Unions (SATU). The Labour Ministry then dissolved the old Trades Union Congress at Kandasamy's request. This was followed by the formation of the National Trades Union Congress (NTUC) led by PAP stalwarts C Devan Nair and Mahmud Awang on September 6, 1961. SATU was deregistered by the authorities in 1963 when its leaders were detained in Operation Coldstore and the NTUC became the only labour movement in Singapore. Kandasamy was a member of the NTUC Central Committee from the start, but he devoted his energies to the union he led: the AUPE. Its ability to negotiate with the government was not lost on others. The junior nurses in government hospitals, who wanted better pay and working conditions, were unhappy with the Singapore Medical Services Union (SMSU). They took their grievances to the AUPE. Keen on amalgamating all public sector unions, AUPE took up their case. It was not smooth sailing. The SMSU filed counter-proposals and the Health Ministry dragged its feet. Fed up with the stalemate, the nurses went on strike on June 7, 1963.

Lee visited the Singapore General Hospital and spoke to the nurses on the first day, but the strike ended only on the sixth day when the government referred the dispute to arbitration. Kandasamy resigned as Parliamentary Secretary to lead the strike. The workers came first to this true-blue unionist. Three months after the strike, Singapore went to the polls on September 21, 1963. Kandasamy, who represented Kampong Kapor, did not contest the elections this time. Instead, he became the full-time general secretary of the AUPE.

Kandasamy resigned as deputy secretary-general of the NTUC in 1965. He disagreed with the the NTUC's decision to back a government move for disciplinary action against an AUPE branch chairman accused of issuing a "defamatory" circular against an "emperor with a hoarse voice" in the Health Ministry.

The AUPE was his heart and soul. He worked closely with his colleagues at the AUPE headquarters in Serangoon Road. After work, he would go with his union friends to some late-night supper joint, where they would chat and joke, before he sent them home. Even over the meal and behind the wheel of his light brown Volkswagen, he would talk about unions and civil servants. The union was his life — and, when he finally got married at the age of 52, the bride was a union member he had fallen in love with.

Lim Kim Choo was a student nurse when he met her during the nurses' agitation. She was a specialist nurse when they got married in England in April 1971. He did not tell even his personal secretary. Ruby Gomez said she found out only a year later. "Kim went to England for a midwife course and came back in 1972. She came to the old office in Serangoon Road, introduced herself to me, and took me out to lunch at Savoy House in Serangoon Plaza. It was only during lunch that she told me she got married in England in April the previous year," she said, talking about her boss to Peter Lim, his biographer.

Kim Choo died of cancer in June 1990 at the age of 47, leaving behind two children: Subhas and Shanti.

Much had changed by then. The days of strikes and agitations were dead and gone, put down by legal reforms such as the Criminal Law (Temporary Provisions) (Amendment) Bill introduced on February 27, 1967. This made it illegal for workers providing essential services to go on strike without a 14-day notice. The government promoted harmony in industrial relations. Tripartism became the official policy promoting collaboration among the employers, employees and the Government for economic growth and all-round benefits. The National Wages Council was formed by the government in February 1972 to formulate wage guidelines. The tripartite body, comprising business, union and government representatives, meets every year to deliberate and seek a national consensus on wages and related issues.

The AUPE has moved from Serangoon Road to Upper Paya Lebar Road, where the spacious, four-storey, Wisma AUPE has been its headquarters since 1972. The union continues to help members and promote good relations between employers and employees.

Kandasamy was AUPE general secretary till 1995 when he was succeeded by his friend and then deputy general secretary, Paul Tan. There was the occasional leadership challenge, such as in 1980, but he beat off the challengers and remained a senior adviser to the union after stepping down as general secretary at the age of 74.

He worked for others as well besides union members. He helped set up the Singapore Indian Education Trust to provide financial assistance to students, served on the Tamils Representative Council and was a trustee of the Singapore Indian Development Association.

He was dismayed with changes to the medical benefits scheme. Civil servants were told they would have to bear part of the cost of their and their dependants' treatment in hospitals and outpatient clinics from January 1994. The unions were briefed on the same day this was announced in Parliament by the then Finance Minister Richard Hu — on November 11, 1993. The union members "could not believe the unions had not been consulted on such a serious matter", the AUPE said in a letter to the Finance Ministry. *The Straits Times* came out with a report headlined "Civil service union rejects new medical benefits plan". The AUPE in a letter to the newspaper protested that the union had not rejected the plan. The then Prime Minister Goh Chok Tong intervened to settle the issue.

That Fellow Kanda, written by Peter Lim, the former editor-in-chief of the Straits Times Press, was published by the AUPE in 1996 after Kandasamy stepped down as general secretary. It was the union's "token of appreciation" for his services. Kandasamy, who died on March 20, 1999, at the age of 77, is fondly remembered by his former colleagues. Ma Wei Cheng, adviser to the AUPE, recalls: "AUPE used to conduct courses when Kandasamy asked me to join him in October 1974, and I ended working for AUPE for 40 years.

"I enjoyed working for him for such a long time because he was very sincere, always doing his best to help workers. We used to work very late into the night. Some of our wives were suspicious of our late-night activities and expressed unhappiness. But Kanda assured them that "when your husbands are with me, they are not up to mischief".

"Many of his colleagues felt that he was able to devote all his time to his work because he was a bachelor boy, unlike others with family commitments. But after his marriage, late in life, he continued to work very hard. "Kanda always wanted to help the lower-income people and he emphasised the importance of education, and for children to help their parents. He supported various community organisations. He also took an interest in studying human behaviour.

"He enjoyed food, especially his favourite dish, nasi padang, at the Glory Indonesia Restaurant in East Coast. Yet he was very health-conscious and used to jog often. During his later years, he used to go for regular walks.

"I recall an incident in the 1960s, when he was very keen to get the Japanese involved in Public Services International (PSI). He was introduced in English by his Japanese counterpart like a good host, who made every effort to ensure that Kanda understood every word he delivered.

"Kanda, on the other hand, gave the impression he did not understand a word of Japanese, acknowledged the compliments in English and then broke out in fluent Japanese, surprising his very appreciative Japanese comrades, who applauded him. He also spoke fluent Malay."

Lee Yoke Lan, former director of nursing, recalls: "Kanda never left anything to chance. He planned and had a strategy before attending meetings to negotiate employee benefits. He would rehearse the entire process.

"He was a good teacher, widely read and eager to impart his knowledge. He was also a good public speaker and very charismatic leader.

"I will never forget the day he spoke fluent Japanese at the PSI conference. I never knew he could speak in Japanese. Throughout his speech, he never uttered a word of English.

"We also had fun working with him. We used to travel in a convoy of cars across the Causeway to picnic at places like Kota Tinggi Waterfalls and Pulau Tioman in Johore. Kanda owned a Volkswagen, which was very popular in the '60s.

Kandasamy offering 'something special' to CV Devan Nair at a dinner event.

"We had potluck when we picnicked, knowing Kanda loved to eat. I was young and a glutton, eating practically anything. Kanda was aware of my insatiable appetite and one day jokingly inquired, "I want to know what you don't like to eat." I told him that the only thing I found unpalatable was the smell of cheese."

"At one outing a colleague brought a pot of chicken curry and he challenged me to finish the entire preparation with bread. I did, which Kanda never expected of me. "Kanda was very generous. He would treat his staff to dinner whenever they worked late.

"I also came to know his parents. Kanda was a very filial son who looked after his parents and his siblings. He was also a very doting father of two lovely children. As a midwife, I felt proud to be the first person to carry his first-born son, Subhas Kim, in my arms. I also knew his sister, Shanti Kim, as a baby."

Recalling the 1963 nurses' strike, she adds: "I was not initially involved in the strike. I only came to know when a nurse stopped me from going to work. I was attached to the Singapore General Hospital.

"Subsequently, I got involved in an advisory capacity, advising nurses to channel their grievances in a judicious manner and not to harass seniors and matrons on their way to work. We sang and played games and I gradually took control of the situation. It was my first experience of a strike.

"I was present when the PM came on the first day of the strike and wanted to deal with a few representatives," she says.

AUPE deputy general secretary Noor Shyma A Latiff says: "I came to know Kanda much later. He was someone whom the workers trusted. He used to drive a hard bargain, always trying to get the best for the workers. He was prepared to negotiate as long as it would take to secure the best deal, once way past midnight. He had a unique strategy. When he was dissatisfied with negotiations, he would lift his bag from the floor, giving the impression that the meeting was concluded and he was packing to leave. And just as everyone heaved a sigh of relief, he would place the bag on the floor and continue negotiating.

"A copper bust of Kandasamy was installed as a tribute to him on the second-level lobby of Wisma AUPE in September 1999," she adds.

So Kandasamy has not left the building yet. And Singapore is Singapore, of course, because of the lawyer he met all those years ago.

BY ABHIJIT NAG

ARMY BUILDER

Kirpa Ram Vij had to flee his home as a child and build a new life for himself in Singapore. He pledged his life to protect his new home as Singapore's first chief of Armed Forces.

Born in 1935 in a hilly village in the Hazara region south of the main Himalayan range, Kirpa and his family were uprooted by the communal bloodbath that followed the partition of India in 1947. They were one of the eight or nine Hindu families living in a predominantly Muslim village of about 200 Pathan families. Life was orderly and enjoyable for young Kirpa, who went about helping his father, a shopkeeper and landowner, until the partition riots. Like most villages in India, Hazara lacked basic facilities and the villagers depended on the nearby running stream, flowing down from the Himalayas and snaking its way south, for their domestic needs. To consume drinking water, Kirpa trudged two to three kilometres each day to fetch treated water from a stand pipe.

Life was very simple and sheltered in the village and the 12-year-old did not know much about Singapore till the onset of partition, where he witnessed the horrors of religious strife between Hindus and Muslims. His family was forced to flee the ancestral home and take refuge in a camp in Delhi for about two months.

There were several transit-camps in Delhi and people were being assimilated with relatives or in settlements that matched their language and customs. It was in one such camp that his father decided against relocating to another village in India and, instead, opted to make a fresh start in the British colony of Singapore.

So he contacted his elder brother, who was in Singapore, to make arrangements to house his family in Singapore. They took a train from Faridabad, near Delhi, to go to Chennai for the voyage to Singapore. During that terrifying train journey, Kirpa saw people going towards or coming across the India-Pakistan border being attacked by members of other religious

Brigadier General Vij with Chief of Army Staff of the Indian Army, Field Marshal Sam Manekshaw.

communities on Grand Trunk Road. He feared for his life and worried where the next meal would come from.

The scars of war left a lasting memory in the young boy — and the humble octogenarian still refers to himself as a refugee to this day.

The journey to Chennai took four to five days. Then they boarded the ship, *SS Rajula*, and sailed to Singapore.

More hardships followed. When the family arrived in Singapore in October 1947, they stayed with 20 others in a small terrace house in Changi Village. His uncle, who immigrated here much earlier, lived in Joo Chiat with his family. He was a contractor providing dhoby (laundry) and tailoring services to the British. They subsequently moved to Kampong Marican before settling into a three-room HDB flat in Owen Road.

Kirpa's father made a modest living by buying items like shoes and clothing from wholesalers and selling them in a pushcart in the vicinity of Arab Street. But he wanted his children to do better and pushed Kripa to study hard and succeed.

And succeed he did. He went on to Raffles Institution, where he was a prefect and a quarter-master in the school cadet corps. He did not want to study beyond school. Instead, he wanted to be a teacher.

"My father was a petty trader and I was the eldest in a family of eight children. It was a question of survival. I wanted to become a teacher to support the family. It was Mr Philip Liau, my form teacher, who advised me to enrol in the university and that changed my life," he says, speaking with quiet dignity in his Seletar Hills home, tastefully decorated by his wife.

As fate would have it, Kirpa missed the deadline to submit his application to become a teacher and so pursued a university degree by default.

After his graduation in 1959, he worked in the Land Office and the Ministry of Finance. But his love of the uniform persisted. He joined the Singapore Volunteer Corps, and took military lessons conducted by the British army. He also frequented its headquarters at Beach Road.

He distinguished himself and was awarded the Sword of Honour in 1960. He was also one of the youngest Singaporeans to be honoured with the Pingat Jasa Gembilang (PJG) during the 1967 National Day Celebrations.

The award boosted his morale and prepared him to confront battle. He was pressed into service during the Confrontation when Indonesia tried to destabilise Malaysia in 1963. He was mobilised as an artillery officer in the Malaysian armed forces and stationed in Johore. He saw action when the artillery bombarded approaching Indonesian infiltrators.

Subsequently, he was also mobilised during Singapore's racial riots in 1964.

In 1965, when Singapore gained independence, he was seconded to the Singapore Armed Forces and became the founding director general of the Singapore Armed Forces Training Institute, (SAFTI) with the directive to build a top-class military school.

Brig. Gen. Kirpa Ram Vij admits that his proudest moment was when the first batch of officers graduated from the newly-established Singapore Armed Forces Training Institute in 1967. And the most challenging? When the army first conducted live firing exercises.

"The first Officer Training Conversion course started with a batch of 37 officers and was multiracial in composition, made up of police officers, teachers and other civilians. These officers later formed the nucleus for mapping out training techniques and learning programmes for new recruits. After commissioning the first batch, we immediately started the second batch," he says.

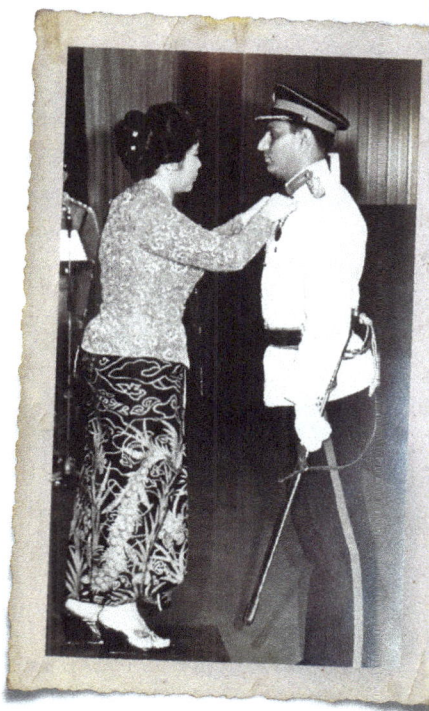

Brigadier General Vij receiving the Meritorious Service Medal (Pingat Jasa Gemilang) from Puan Noor Aishah Singapore, 1967.

"Most of the training methods were learnt from Israeli officers and focused on physical and mental training. We did not have the basic training equipment found in a gym, hence the method of training was very simple and concentrated more on route training. Often we had to improvise, like using a boat shed to train in Pasir Laba Camp, when we discovered that we could run from Jurong Road down a dirt track to the sea and back.

"Things happened very fast and worked very well. We had a good team of officers and we had to learn and implement at the same time," he says.

"At that time, Singapore's military officers were sent to the Jungle Warfare School in Kota Tinggi, in Johore for training. It was part and parcel of an agreement sealed by the British," he adds.

He was appointed commander of the first National Service Brigade in 1969 and nine months later became the first director of the Command and Staff College. The following year, he became Director, General Staff (head of army), a post he held for four years.

On his return to the administrative service, he held several key positions before being posted as ambassador to Egypt in 1975 for four years. At the same time, he was accredited to Yugoslavia, Lebanon and Pakistan. While covering Pakistan, he revisited his village in Hazara and found that the serene and unspoilt scenery he had left behind no longer existed.

"It was completely different from the one I left. Rising high on the cloistered hills where my house once stood was the Tarbella dam. My village, school and other landmarks no longer existed," he laments.

After returning to Singapore, he held leading positions in several organisations, including the general manager of Neptune Orient Lines from 1981 to 1995.

Commenting on his successful career spanning 45 years, he says, "I had four jobs and each one was completely different from the other. My policy is that you should put your heart and soul into whatever you have been assigned to do, just as an able student who takes over from a teacher."

It appears that Kirpa will not stop moving. He has just moved into a new home in Arcadia Road and is once again looking forward to a new beginning.

BY ALFRED DASS

SPORTS AFICIONADO

SS Dhillon's passion for sports carried him through a career that placed value and virtue of service before self.

athiavan Singh Dhillon, the first secretary-general of Singapore National Olympic Council was born in Perak, Lumut, in 1931. He lived there until the age of three, when the family moved to Taiping, a district in Perak. His father, a Malayan by birth, was chief clerk in the public works department in Taiping. Looking calm and relaxed in his home, surrounded by lush greenery in Arcadia Road, he said, "Life was beautiful and going to school and sitting for examinations was a pleasure".

He grew up in a large family with four brothers and four sisters and enjoyed his childhood until he was 10. He was doing well at King Edward VII School in Taiping. As a young boy, he spent his time in rural surroundings listening to the sounds of myriad birds chirping and passed his time catching fish in a nearby stream. He was living in an oasis of calm until the Japanese invaded Malaya in 1941. He witnessed British officers retreating towards Singapore, from marauding Japanese forces charging on foot and on bicycles from the north.

The family retreated to a safe and discreet estate in Padang Rengas, where his father owned 30 acres of fruit and rubber plantations. "Markets were closed and vegetables were scarce. So we had to be self-sustaining and planted vegetables for ourselves," he remarked. He was never afraid of dirtying his hands and lent a hand, planting vegetables.

Three months later, when the British surrendered, the family travelled 22 miles in three bullock carts and returned to their village in Taiping. The family was lucky and not tortured by the Japanese, and neither did he witness any atrocities by Japanese soldiers.

However, upon his return to King Edward VII School, he learnt that he had to study Japanese, and all his lessons were to be taught in Japanese.

During interval and after school, students had to sing Japanese military and folk songs. Young Dhillon found it all very boring and, one day during recess, he left school and never returned. He took to farm life and passed his time in his one-acre home, spending hours in the garden and tending to the two ponies on the farm, which the Japanese soldiers eventually took away and caused him much sadness.

To earn a living, the family began farming and sold milk, butter and other staples. Farm life continued for four years, until he heard the British and Indian soldiers were returning.

He went back to King Edward VII School in 1945 and found that he had forgotten what he had learnt in English. He could no longer even read English. It had become unfamiliar to him because the Japanese had destroyed all the English books. However, he picked up the language and remembered the old lessons within a month.

He lost four years of education because of the Japanese Occupation, and sat for his "O" Levels when he was 19. His Scottish headmaster, JD Joseph, who was promoted to principal of Teachers Training College (TTC) in Singapore, invited students to apply to the TTC if they wanted to be teachers.

Dhillon sent in his application and was interviewed at the TTC in Cairnhill Road in December 1951. He began training in March the following year. As part of the Normal Teacher Training Course, he was posted to Bukit Panjang Government Primary School. Minister Vivian Balakrishnan's parents taught at the school, he recalls.

After teaching, he attended lectures at the TTC to prepare for his year-end exams. After completing the three-year course, he qualified to be a teacher in 1955 and was transferred to Birkhall School, in Margaret Road. "I was now staying in High Street, where Parliament House stands, and as a qualified teacher I was paid $200 a month."

12 April 1959 marked an important date in his life, when he returned to Ipoh to get married. It also marked a turning point in his career. He was posted to Monks Hill School in Newton where he taught art, history, physical education (PE), and became the sports secretary. "My two daughters were growing up and I needed to sustain a family. So I started teaching night classes known as Lembaga Gerakan Pelajaran Dewasa (Adult Education Board) in Raffles Institution, to supplement my income. I also decided that I should improve myself and applied to Loughborough College, London, to study physical education in sport.

"Although it was a three-year course, I was exempted for two years because of my past experience in sports. I completed the one-year course within 10 months and obtained my Diploma in Physical Education. "While I was in England, I officiated at athletic meets and refereed rugby matches during weekends. I was not paid for my services, and did it for the joy." Later, he would become a well-known referee who officiated at many games at the Padang.

Mr Dhillon receiving the highest award from the United States Sports Academy for his contribution to sports.

While in England, he became qualified to judge all athletic events and several field sports such as football, hockey and cricket. He is also a certified time keeper accredited by the Loughborough College Athletic Club.

He returned to Singapore in 1966 and was posted to the Ministry of Education to be a physical education (PE) inspector. As part of his new job, he advised schools in the City District, such as Raffles Institution and Victoria Schools, to set up rugby, soccer and PE programmes. He was a keen sportsman and dedicated all seven days to sports and outdoor activities. His favourite sports were rugby and cricket.

In early 1970, Dhillon heard about the National Stadium being built and the setting up of the Singapore National Olympic Council. In December 1970, when the SNOC advertised the position of secretary-general, he was holidaying in Perak where he received a telegram about the new job.

Joseph David, his superior, encouraged him to apply for the post. Dhillon followed his advice and was eventually selected to become the first SNOC secretary-general in 1971. He started operations in a small office with one clerk, and an office table with four chairs, in Sports House in Farrer Park.

Given only limited resources, one of his challenges was to look for funds to earn his salary. He held charitable events and dinners to raise funds. EW Barker, former minister for law and president of the Singapore National Olympic Council (SNOC), also secured funds from the Singapore Turf Club.

Dhillon's first task was leading the Singapore contingent to the 1972 Munich Olympics, where the infamous massacre of Israeli athletes took place. He recalled hearing the gunfire but dismissed it, thinking athletes were burning firecrackers to celebrate their victories. Then Singapore's golden girl, Patricia Chan, came dashing to tell him about the terrorist raid and firing of bullets. He subsequently followed the entire episode on TV and, as chef de mission, reported the incident to his superiors when he returned to Singapore.

Although Dhillon retired in 1996 after serving for half a century, his passion for sports still lingers and he regularly attends sporting events with his wife. The 80-year-old, whose appearance belies his age, gets up in the wee hours of the morning to catch live telecasts of international football matches. He also spends time with his eight grandchildren playing lawn bowls at the Singapore Cricket Club.

Dhillon's greatest satisfaction is that he has won recognition from former President SR Nathan and Prime Minister Lee Hsien Loong. He considers that more valuable than money.

BY MARY LEE AND ABHIJIT NAG

BORN TO RUN

Sergit Singh was only 15 when he became the first
Singaporean schoolboy to run the 800 metres in under
two minutes, but it hasn't been roses, roses all the way.

O ne can hardly blame Sergit Singh for being bitter about his life. Born in 1953, he
showed athletic promise in school, but the sporting infrastructure simply did not
exist at that time to help talents like him. The road to success was strewn with
hurdles. Sergit was only 15 when he blitzed into the record books. He earned "the distinction
of being the first Singapore schoolboy athlete to run the 800 metres in under two minutes",
according to *The Straits Times*.

He set that record in his very first competition — at the national schools athletics
championships at the Farrer Park Athletics Track, on July 11, 1969. The record remained
unbroken for 18 years. Four years after that record run, he made the news again when he won
a bronze medal in the 1973 Southeast Asian Peninsular Games in Singapore.

He had his moments in the sun, but heartbreaks too. Life hasn't been kind to Sergit. One
of his daughters committed suicide aged 12 when she failed to qualify for the PSLE express
stream. He himself had a stroke three weeks after suddenly giving up smoking. Sergit, who
smoked for 40 years, said his doctor told him that he should have quit gradually.

There were other false steps. Off the field, he fell into bad company in his youth.
Growing up in the 1970s, when the drug culture was at its height, it was difficult for a teen
like him to resist its lure. He became one of the many victims.

He wasn't a good student and didn't do well in any of his subjects, but he strove to
excel like any highflyer in his chosen field — the school field. Relentlessly, he pounded the
tracks, like a runner possessed. He didn't need any competitor, any running mate, to give his
best. Out alone in the sweltering sun, he raced against the clock. Faster and faster, he was
determined to run — every practice run had to be faster than the one before.

To gain more speed and stamina, he even ran after teacher C Kunalan's bike after school. That was part of his training, too. Funny incidents sometimes happened during training. "I remember one day when we were training in the beautiful Naval Base and were chased by a black dog trying to protect her newborn puppies," he said. "We ran for our lives — and after the frightening episode joked that perhaps that dog chase helped us enhance our performance."

"But", he added, "we were disappointed that we would not be able to train in the same picturesque surroundings and decided that the only way to reclaim our territory was to chase the dog away. So the next day when we saw her, we charged towards her. Terrified, the dog turned tail and starting running towards a metal fence. Seeing her wriggling between the fence, we took deep breaths and started barking furiously at the her. From that day on, she never chased us."

He wanted to help others become athletes, too, and gathered a group of boys, spending hours training them. They formed an athletics team to compete under the banner of the Singapore Tamil Association. Athletics and sports governing bodies initially refused to allow the team to compete under the banner of the Tamil Association as it was a cultural organisation. However, they relented when they found the team was cosmopolitan. It also had an Englishman who was from the ANZUK forces.

Sergit thinks it was one of the best teams to emerge in this region, for it had won several major competitions in Singapore and Malaysia in the 800-metre, 1,500-metre and 1,600-metre categories. It beat more well-known teams like the Singapore Armed Forces and Swifts in the Singapore Amateur Athletics Association road relay event. According to him, his team broke the national record in the 4 x 1,600 metres.

The race is not to the swift, however. After the cheers and the medals, the athletes return to normal life — and often fade away. Records are broken, past winners forgotten.

Sergit concluded, rather wistfully: "Perhaps there must be a paradigm shift in the way we reward athletes. We need to assure them lifetime career opportunities and support. Perhaps giving them a pension in their twilight years and caring for them when they suffer from disabilities or injuries will help, for sportspeople tend to be more prone to injuries due to vigorous training."

Sergit is a devout follower of Sathya Sai Baba and believes faith is helping him overcome his stroke.

BY VEENA BHARWANI

THE SILAT CHAMPION

Champions are made, not born. Just ask Sheik Ala'uddin, a skinny little kid who grew into a mighty silat star.

He was a small, scrawny child. Sheik Ala'uddin was not born to be a silat star. Football was his favourite sport as a boy. However, a chance encounter with a religious teacher when he was 15 rerouted him to the prestigious martial art. He was at the Aleem Siddique Mosque in Lorong K, Telok Kurau one day to meet his friends. They were planning to form a football team.

But that was not to be. They chanced upon a mosque representative who impressed upon them the importance of attending religious classes instead of playing football. Not long after the same representative mentioned silat classes to them — and a week later introduced the boys to a silat exponent dressed in a bright green ceremonial uniform.

Sheik Ala'uddin did not turn into a silat star overnight. His story is one of hardship and hard work with a dollop of pain as well.

"I was very scrawny, shy and nervous and, during my first session, I found out that I did not have the physical strength for the sport," he recalled.

As he plunged headlong into a gruelling regime of silat training, he became more motivated. First, he started training five times a week and then he upped it to a daily routine. "My body started to build up I became more encouraged. Then I decided to set up my own training room in my home, where my late Mother kindly gave me space. My home was located near Pachitan, where the Gurkha contingent is. I named the training room Sanga Juara or House of Champion." While his training intensified, the lad still had no ambitions of being a champion.

For one, he was a late starter. He began at 15 while kids now start at three. However, the "can do" spirit kept him going. He started competitive training in 1984 and his first competition the same year. In 1985, he competed in both fights and artistic categories. He never gave in to his initial nervousness. When he entered the ring, the fear disappeared and he stood a self-confident man who seemed to be able to get the better of his opponents. Encouraged by his wins, he poured all his energy on his fitness.

But his lack of money threatened his stint as a Silat exponent. He refused to quit and found a way to fuel his passion for the martial art. "I had no money to buy a proper training bench. So I took planks covering a drain to make my own weight training bench. I was determined to get stronger. I also bought body-enhancing supplements from the Chinese sinseh, which I discovered made my urine green. People who noticed my urine colour gave me strange looks. I was very ignorant about supplements then and practically bought anything to build up my body," he said. Gradually, his weight increased from 65 kg in 1965 to a burly 100 kg in 1985.

For a Silat fighter, he was still considered very skinny in the early days. So he decided to join a gym — the New Bre International Gym at Katong — paying a $40 monthly membership fee. Rahmat Juhami, Mr Singapore and Mr Asia, who worked out in the gym, helped him train. As his body toned up, so did his confidence and self-esteem along with his knowledge of *silat*.

You wouldn't think a fighter like him had any fears, but he did fear the glaring lights of the media. He suffered a total shutdown when he faced cameras or girls. No one in those days was taught how to handle the media. But the man had a plan. He came up with the concept of "bulldozing" himself — *terjok betul* in Malay. He would say yes to any task. And, from then on, he bulldozed into victory in many areas.

He was a man who didn't know how to say no. He said yes to becoming a fitness instructor. He organised fitness competitions, body building shows and 30-storey vertical marathons in HDB estates.

"I reckon I was the first to initiate vertical marathon in Singapore," he said.

As a boy growing in a kampong, he was infused with a "can do it and doing it better" spirit which became his mantra.

Silat gave him the strength and daredevil attitude to try out new things. "People started noticing me and soon others too adopted this attitude," he recalled.

His daredevil attitude aside, life for him was very tough financially. He took on a variety of jobs to make ends meet and feed his passion. He was a bouncer, a cargo breaker at SATS and a cashier at Far East plaza at one point. He overworked himself to pay for his bike, health supplements and training equipment. This overwork finally took a toll on him as he became ill and vomited one day. Still, "no" was not in his vocabulary.

After winning the 1990 World Silat Championships in Holland for Singapore, the then 23-year old beat a field of 20 competitors in the 80-85 kg category. He was basking in the limelight and began to overcome his camera-shyness. He won consecutive gold medals between 1991 and 1999 at the SEA Games. To add to his collection of golds in the SEA Games, he won other competitions; the 1992 International Thailand Open Championships, the 1994 Pencak Silat World Invitational Championships, the 1996 Malaysia National Championships and the International Philippines Open Championships in 1999.

He is a man who doesn't say no to any challenge. He has instilled the same attitude in his six kids. The man believes in action. "Just do it", he says. And, considering all he has achieved, one can only say: "Well done!"

BY ABHIJIT NAG

PHYSICIAN FIRST

Dr BR Sreenivasan played a notable role as a physician and was the first vice-chancellor of the University of Singapore.

H e was the first vice-chancellor of the University of Singapore. Dr Baratham Ramaswamy Sreenivasan, however, preferred to be known as a family physician. Dr Sreenivasan was clearly a man with a calling. He continued to work for better health care and better training for doctors long after his brief but eventful stewardship of the university.

The dignity of high office could not tie down the independent-minded doctor, who stepped down as vice-chancellor after a dispute with the government in 1963. He might not have gotten his way as vice-chancellor, but he made his influence felt in other spheres. He had his say on the decolonisation of the public service, wanting foreigners replaced with locals; and, as a founder member of the Singapore Anti-Tuberculosis Association (SATA), he took part in the battle to eradicate the biggest killer disease of the time.

Born on June 14, 1909, in Gemas, Malaya, he was the son of a cashier and a landowner's daughter. He was educated at St John's Institution, Kuala Lumpur, and qualified in medicine in 1931 at the King Edward VII College of Medicine, Singapore.

After the outbreak of World War II and during Japanese Occupation, he served as a medical officer at the civil general hospital.

Amid the horrors unleashed by the war was a rise in tuberculosis (TB). Before the war, TB was mainly a disease that plagued the labouring classes, but the middle and upper classes too began to fall victim during and after the war.

Dr Sreenivasan, who specialised in treating the disease and became the chief medical officer of Tan Tock Seng Hospital, gave a talk to doctors in January 1947, calling for more TB treatment facilities.

Soon after, a group of eminent people and doctors called a public meeting to discuss the formation of an association to prevent TB. Finally, on August 23, 1947, the Singapore Anti-Tuberculosis Association (SATA) was officially launched and duly registered by the colonial government. Dr Sreenivasan was among the founder members.

In 1953, he became a Member of the Royal College of Physicians (MRCP) and later elected a Fellow. From 1954 to 1957 he was president of the Medical Council of Singapore.

In 1955, Singapore's then chief minister, David Marshall, established a Malayanisation Commission with Dr Sreenivasan as chairman. The commission was asked to recommend measures for "rapid, systematic and complete Malayanisation of the public service" (which was then largely run by the British), wrote Kevin Tan in *Marshall of Singapore: A Biography*. In March 1956, the commission published its report.

The majority report urged rapid Malayanisation, starting with the Administrative Service, while the minority report restated the British position that the higher echelons should be Malayanised only gradually.

Subsequently, Dr Sreenivasan also looked into government expenditure. In July 1960, he was named head of a six-man commission of inquiry into recurrent government expenditure for "increasing the efficiency of government administration and reducing the mounting cost of running the public service", *The Straits Times* reported, quoting the finance ministry.

Dr BR Sreenivasan chatting with delegates at the Third National Medical Convention.

Yang Di-Pertuan Negara Yusof Ishak being presented with the First Interim Report of the Inquiry into Government Expenditure Commission at the Istana Negara, by Chairman of the Commission Dr BR Sreenivasan.

The doctor also liked to teach and got involved in university affairs years before he became vice-chancellor. He was a member of the committee whose report led to the establishment of the two autonomous divisions of the University of Malaya in Singapore and Kuala Lumpur in 1959. He was an honorary teacher in the Faculty of Medicine when in 1961 he was appointed principal of the Singapore division of the University of Malaya. When the University of Singapore became a separate entity in 1962, he assumed charge as vice-chancellor.

He entertained grand visions of the university. On June 14, 1962, *The Straits Times* reported him as saying the best investment Singapore could make would be to plough money into the expansion of the university. The university, which then had 2,247 students, must admit more students, he said. He also stressed the need for research to attract scholars from all over the world.

Those were troubled times, however. On February 2, 1963, Operation Coldstore was launched — a security operation in which at least 111 anti-government left-wing activists were arrested and detained, including key members of the opposition political party, *Barisan Sosialis*. Others arrested included newspaper editors, trade unionists and university students.

Dr Sreenivasan was drawn into the fray. The government wanted the university to bar students suspected of being subversive. Dr Sreenivasan objected to this, seeing it as political interference and an infringement of university autonomy. "The government then intimated that funds required for the university's development plans would be delayed, prompting the intransigent vice-chancellor to resign," according to the book, *The University Socialist Club and the Contest for Malaya*, authored by Loh Kah Seng, Edgar Liao, Lim Cheng Tju and Seng Guo-Quan.

Dr Sreenivasan resumed his career as a family physician after he resigned as vice-chancellor. In 1973, he was made a fellow of the Royal College of General Practitioners, of which he was a founder member. He was also the founder president of the Singapore College of General Practitioners, officially inaugurated on June 30, 1971. "Speaking on the objectives of the two-year old college, he said GPs had to know the most recent advances in medicine and that was why the college was formed," reported *The Straits Times*, quoting him, on March 25, 1973. He stressed the importance of GPs, pointing out they were the physicians usually consulted by patients before being referred to specialists.

The doctor, whose favourite hobby was walking, may have receded from public memory since his death on May 23, 1977. But there is no denying he was a notable figure in his time. "His love of Shakespeare made him the complete physician, caring both for the body and spirit of his patients," wrote EK Koh in the *Journal of the Royal College of General Practitioners* in August 1977. "He was so knowledgeable, so witty and yet so humble," marvelled Koh.

References

Royal College of Physicians, Lives of the Fellows, Munk's Roll, Volume VII, Baratham Ramaswamy Sreenivasan, http://munksroll.rcp ondon.ac.uk/Biography/Details/4203

The SATA Story, Celebrating 65 Years of Caring for The Community, 2012, http:/www.sata.com.sg/wp-content/uploads/2014/09 SATA-e-book_v7_9Oct12_FINAL.pdf

The Straits Times, March 8, 1961, pp6

BY ABHIJIT NAG

NATURE'S TRUE CHILD

"Most of the world wants to see nature, but not to be immersed in it," said Subaraj Rajathurai, Singapore's first professional tourist guide specialising in eco-tourism.

With a flowing beard, a bandanna around his head, in T-shirt and jeans, he looked like a musician or an artist. He is however, a true nature's child, dedicated to showing and preserving the vestiges of wilderness in Singapore. Subaraj Rajathurai, better known as Raj or Sub, is Singapore's first professional tourist guide specialising exclusively in eco-tourism. "I created a profession in Singapore," he said, referring to the others who have followed in his footsteps. Licensed by the Singapore Tourism Board since 1990, he has more than 20 years of experience professionally guiding birdwatchers from around the world. He can take you around Southeast Asia — or Sungei Buloh.

"Singapore's a small place but what we have is convenience," he said, pointing out this is one place where tourists can visit shopping malls and nature reserves on the same day. "Most of the world wants to see nature, but not to be immersed in it," he added.

As a tourist guide, he has an interest in preserving what's left of Mother Nature in Singapore, of course. But it's not just business for him. He has had a thing about birds and nature since childhood.

When children in his neighbourhood were outdoors playing catch, cops and robbers, hide and seek, catching spiders, he was flipping through magazines, hunting for pictures of animals, that he painstakingly compiled in a scrapbook. "To me, my scrapbook was like my family album, as I felt the same joy as those who relive family albums," he said.

According to him, each animal in his album told a story. He kept his album at his bedside and he would "read" himself to sleep. Born on April 16, 1963, Subaraj grew up in Siglap and studied in Guillemard East Primary School, which no longer exists. He remembers the three-storey building and its lush surroundings.

"There were many trees surrounding my school and I was easily distracted by the chirping of birds. I would pause from whatever I was doing, even when I was playing during recess. There were many colourful butterflies that visited the various flowering bushes at school and I would search for jumping (fighting) spiders and "click" beetles with my friends. Following heavy rain, two of my favourite things to do were sliding about playing football and looking for tadpoles in the rain pools, both on the school field. At home, though we had only a small garden at our terrace house, there was a world of insects and other invertebrates to discover and observe."

From Guillemard East, he went on to Tanjong Katong Secondary School and then dropped out of Stamford College. "I quit when asked to dissect a frog," he said.

Subaraj, whose grandparents were Tamils from Jaffna in Sri Lanka, was lucky — and he knows it. "In our country if you didn't become a graduate, if you didn't have a degree, if you didn't become a doctor, engineer, lawyer, you were a rotter," he said. "But my parents realised I had a sense of direction and they enjoyed their later life with me." They realised he had a passion for nature and did not press him to continue his studies or get a 9-to-5 job.

He had his moment of self-discovery when he went on his first nature trip to Bukit Timah Nature Reserve with his college classmates in 1981. "It was like finding home," he said. That gave him purpose and a sense of direction. He enjoyed reading Gerald Durrell and watching the documentaries made by David Attenborough and Jacques Cousteau. Now, increasingly, he was drawn to the library to do research on wildlife. He joined the Nature Society in 1985 and began taking visiting birdwatchers on professional tours in 1988. "I enjoyed it so much. So, in 1990, I signed up to do the Singapore Tourism Board course for tour guides," he added.

He was also involved in conserving and surveying natural habitats. He spent eight months with three others writing proposals to turn Sungei Buloh into a bird sanctuary. The Government consulted international experts and the Sungei Buloh Nature Park was officially opened in December 1993 by the then prime minister, Goh Chok Tong. It eventually became the Sungei Buloh Wetland Reserve, gazetted as a nature reserve on January 1, 2002.

The Nature Society also persuaded the Government not to destroy a patch of mature forest in the Lower Peirce water catchment for a golf course.

Subaraj is happy the Government is taking steps to enhance the natural habitats in Pulau Ubin. "When you go to Pulau Ubin, you are completely de-stressed," he said. "It is the alter ego to Sentosa." Sentosa is "Fantasy Island", "man-made", while Pulau Ubin is "authentic".

When Prime Minister Lee Hsien Loong visited the island in November 2014, newspapers showed him smiling, holding a thin green snake in his hands. "I gave him the snake," said Subaraj. Others were concerned, but it was a harmless Oriental whip snake, he added. The Prime Minister looked happy and it made to the papers.

Subaraj knows what the media wants: "Over the years the press has approached me for all kinds of stories and I am happy to give my two cents' worth. Let the people benefit from it. That gives me satisfaction." "You have to work with the Government and give it credit," he added. "That's the way to get things done."

He sipped a rose syrup as he spoke, cooling down after being out in the sun at the Dairy Farm with Singapore American School students.

Besides conducting tours, he is also involved in research and consultancy projects with the National University of Singapore and other organisations. "I am following my dream," he said, doing what he loves.

The man who can whistle like a bird also has children answering to the names of birds. Subaraj and his wife, Shamla, married since 1994, wanted their sons to be named after birds. But not just any birds. The names had to sound ethnic, in keeping with their Tamil heritage. So their elder son is named Serin and the younger, Saker. Serin, 19, is named after a species of finch and Saker, 14, after a species of falcon. Luckily, the boys have taken to birdwatching, too, like their parents. Talk about birds of a feather flocking together, it's all in the family for Sub and Sham.

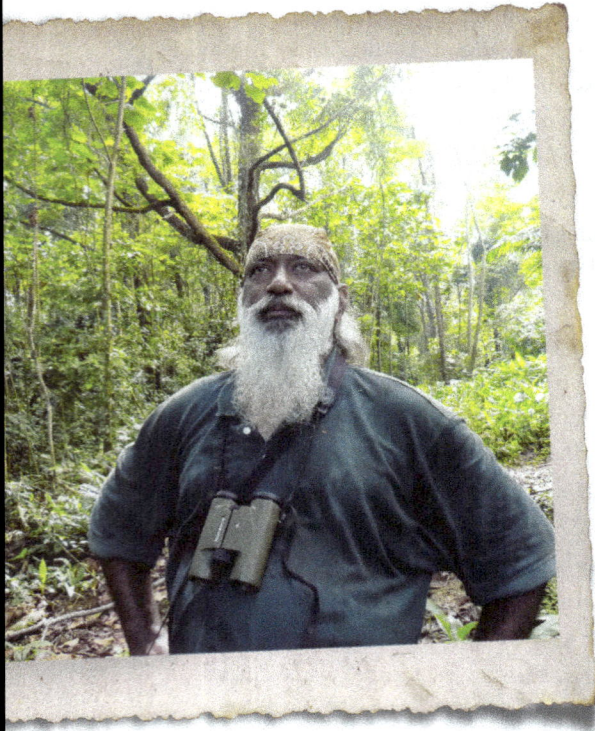

He believes it is the cause of each and every citizen on planet earth to preserve, treasure and protect our precious environment.

BY ABHIJIT NAG

DREAM RUN

Malacca-born PC Suppiah ran for Singapore to be a
Singaporean and it took him all the way to the Olympics.

A kampong boy, he ran for the nation even before he became a citizen. The whip-thin teenager was chasing a dream to be a Singapore citizen. More than medals and a place on the podium, what he wanted was a Singapore passport. PC Suppiah ran for Singapore to be a Singaporean and, dream fulfilled, ran on, crossing milestone after milestone, running barefoot in the Olympics, setting national records, earning glory for himself.

Looking not a day older than 45, the 65-year-old former long-distance runner recalled, "I wanted to play soccer. But I was told the best way to get citizenship was to show individually I was the best. In soccer I couldn't show that. It's a team sport. So I was advised to take up athletics." That put him on the track to fame.

Born in Malacca in 1949, he was seven years old when his father, an engineer, had a stroke and died in his late 30s. His mother, who was 27 years old, returned to Singapore with her six children to live with her parents. They lived in a kampong in the Thomson Road area.

"My mum loved me very much," said Suppiah, the first male child born after two girls in a family of three boys and three girls. To make ends meet, his mother used to give tuitions in Tamil. Suppiah ran errands for the neighbours. "I used to run and fetch things for them. They would give me five cents, 10 cents. We lived opposite the Polo Club in Thomson Road. I had a black dog and used to jog in the club." He made friends there and was allowed to groom the horses. "They gave me some money. One horse owner said I could gallop the horses. I was 14 or 15 then. Each day they would give me a dollar to gallop the horses. In the evening I used to play soccer."

Suppiah, who attended Braddell Primary School before going to Thomson Secondary School, used to win races in school, but soccer was his first love. He was persuaded to train as an athlete by a man named Kartar Singh, whom he met as a schoolboy in 1964. Singh, who was a member of Swift Club, used to coach his son, Aftar Singh, who studied in Anglo-Chinese School. Suppiah and his footballer friends were resting under a tree after a game one day when Singh came in a car with his family. He asked who among them was the fastest runner. When the other boys pointed at Suppiah, Singh asked him to run with his son, saying running would build up his stamina. Singh began coming every other day to see him run with his son, buying him food and vitamins to make him stronger. "Later, I realised he wanted a pacer for his son," said Suppiah.

But he had a reason to continue training under Singh. His school fees had gone up after independence because he was not a Singaporean. Singh then met his mother and said he could become a citizen if he excelled as an athlete.

In January 1966, he took part in a cross-country run at MacRitchie organised by the Singapore Amateur Athletics Association. Running barefoot, he finished fourth. "Everybody was shocked," he recalled, because he was a complete outsider. Two months later, he took part in inter-club athletics at Farrer Park, where the celebrated coach, Maurice Nicholas, asked Singh to let him train the youngster. That is how Nicholas became Suppiah's coach.

Suppiah began winning local events and took part in competitions in Malaysia, Thailand and the Philippines. In 1969, he was selected for the Southeast Asian Peninsular (SEAP) Games in Rangoon. He was only 19. "Everybody came to see me off at the airport. My mother hugged and kissed me." He finished fourth in the 10,000 metres. But the citizenship he sought still eluded him. He had to be 21, he was told.

On his 21st birthday on August 10, 1970, he reminded his coach he wanted to be a citizen. When he qualified for the 1971 SEAP Games in Kuala Lumpur, he refused to go unless he was made a citizen. Nicholas told him not to spoil his chances; he had to go and prove himself.

He went to Kuala Lumpur but was so unhappy he left the camp without telling anyone before the Games opened. His team mate, A Kunalan, who had won the bronze in the 50-metre walk in Rangoon but was also not a citizen, took him to his house in Selangor.

Their disappearance caused a stir. "Maurice cried," said Suppiah, when they returned. He found himself face to face with EW Barker, the Cabinet Minister and president of the Singapore National Olympic Council. The Minister gave him the citizenship papers and said: "I'm going to watch your race and see how good you are."

Suppiah recalled: "I cried and said, 'Sorry, sir, I will do my best.'" The next day, he ran the race of his life. He was running third with four laps remaining, moved up to second position with two laps to go, and then the Burmese front-runner made a mistake. "He turned back every 10 metres. So I knew that he was not strong enough. I ran all out and overtook him in the last 100 metres. I won the gold medal."

"Mr EW Barker came down from the grandstand and he hugged me. He said: "You are my citizen, you are my Olympian, you are the best sportsman of the year." Suppiah, who also took the silver in the 5,000 metres in Kuala Lumpur, won the 1971 Sportsman of the Year award.

In the 1972 Munich Olympics, he attracted attention as a barefoot runner. His picture was plastered around the Olympic Village and sportswear sponsors offered him free shoes.

Munich was marred by the September 5 massacre when Palestinian militants entered the Games village and killed 11 Israeli Olympic team members before they themselves were killed or captured by the German police. Suppiah, however, returned from Munich with a personal achievement. Running against stars like Emiel Puttemans of Belgium and David Bedford of Britain in the 10,000 metres, he became the first Singaporean to break the 32-minute barrier.

After the Olympics, he won a silver in the 5,000 metres in the 1973 SEAP Games in Singapore. Later that year, he set a new national record, running 10,000 metres in 31 minutes and 19 seconds in Manila. No Singaporean could beat that record for 41 years. Finally, 22-year-old undergraduate Soh Rui Yong shaved three seconds off that record in Portland, Oregon, in June 2014.

Looking back, Suppiah happily pointed out his three unique achievements: "I am the only long-distance Olympic runner from Singapore. I am the only long-distance Singaporean gold medallist in the SEA Games. I am the only long-distance runner to win the Sportsman of the Year award."

The former champion, who worked for Singapore Pools from 1971 till 2011, now lives in Kuala Lumpur, where he is general manager of a property firm active in Malaysia and Chennai, India. Athletes should be given jobs and financial assistance to help them rise to international levels, he says. Sportsmen should not be asked to retire, he added. "They bring glory to the company."

Suppiah, the doting father, with his daughter Sugeeta.

He is still active in Singapore Masters Athletics, an organisation for veteran athletes

Trim and dapper, he explained how he has kept himself young. "I don't drink, I don't smoke," he said. "I drink plenty of milk and eat selectively. I run and do my exercise. I jog at least half an hour a day. I don't bring work home and I go to bed early."

"I have to be careful," he added. "My eldest sister died of diabetes when she was 42 years old. My youngest brother also died of diabetes when he was only 40."

Then he smiled, full of life, handing his business card. "Call me any time," he said, ending the interview. "It was a gift from God, my mum's blessing, and I had will power," he concluded, looking back on his glory days.

"I have known PC Suppiah as a schoolboy advancing into a teenager and later into adulthood. He is really an unsung hero of long-distance running," said LTC (Retd) Kesavan Soon, vice-patron of Singapore Athletics and vice-president of Olympians Singapore. "In the 1950s and 60s, the long-distance events were always won by foreigners — mostly from the Commonwealth forces based in Singapore. He was the first local boy to take over command of this event.

"He was the SAAA Sportsman of the Year in 1971 and 1972 and SAFSA Sportsman of the Year in 1974 and 1975. He had won race after race in the gruelling 5,000 metres and 10,000 metres. With all these accolades, Suppiah remained humble and friendly in his outlook and a great inspiration to the younger athletes."

BY ALFRED DASS

DANCING IN THE RING

Boxing is a performing art, says Syed Abdul Kadir, the sole Singaporean to have boxed in the Olympics for Singapore.

T he word "retire" does not seem to exist for this sprightly 67-year-old whose youthful looks belie his age. He looks 15 years younger and moves with the same agility and his trademark sideburns are as bushy as ever — inspired by his idol and the King of Rock 'n' Roll, Elvis Presley, whom he admired for his style. He found Elvis more interesting to watch than listen.

During the interview, his phone kept ringing; two young teenage girls walked in to inquire where they could learn boxing; a photographer from a tabloid asked him to pose for a picture; and he has to acknowledge a business delivery. He attended to everyone and everything with ease. He looked warm and friendly — without the hint of aggression you would expect from a boxer. But Syed Abdul Kadir is in a class of his own — Singapore's one and only boxing Olympian. You can see the scar above his right eye where he caught a nasty nick during the 1972 Munich Olympics.

The former Southeast Asian Peninsular (SEAP) Games boxing champion extolled his sport. "Boxing is not about striking your opponent," he said. "It is about mastering an art to avoid taking punches and exchanging punches skilfully to floor your opponent. And that is one of the main reasons I took up boxing. There is a rhythm in the way you move to duck, sidestep, avoid or throw punches. It is a performing art and it was this beauty that influenced me to take up boxing."

Kadir runs his own boxing school, supervises coaches in the Singapore national team and is president of the Singapore Amateur Boxing Association. He owes everything to the sport, including his wife. They met after he struck gold at the SEAP Games and got married two years after the Olympics.

Kadir represented Singapore in the SEAP Games from 1969 to 1979, winning one gold and two silver medals, and a bronze in New Zealand — Singapore's first bronze Commonwealth Games boxing medal — in 1974.

Incidentally, his son, Syed Muhammed Fahmy, also became a boxing champion.

Boxing, according to Kadir, is a gentleman's sport, if you compete in the true spirit of the game. However, if you see it as a "fight", you will not enjoy it. It is not about delivering hard-hitting blows and raw punches. It is how you deliver them and, in return, receive them without hurting yourself. And, like in any sport, you won't get hurt if you are physically fit. Take soccer, for example, you must be physically fit to take the hard tackles. Similarly, in boxing you won't be hurt if you are fully fit. Sometimes the emotional pain can hurt more than the physical pain, added Kadir.

"Boxing is different from other sports because you engage your opponent very closely, within reach, which is something I found very challenging," he said. "Within that confined space you have to make split-second decisions and employ creative techniques to win. You have to have the sixth sense to anticipate your opponent's next move. And, unlike in some other sports, you don't have the time to recoup and recover if you make a mistake. For instance, in team games like soccer, you can depend on your teammates while you take a breather for a few seconds. But in boxing you depend on yourself and every second counts, a deciding factor in winning or losing a match."

And what gave him his greatest satisfaction in a fight? "It's not so much about winning, but knowing that I gave it my best shot.

"Naturally, every boxer strives to win. When I enter the ring, I don't harbour any feelings towards my opponent. I just psyche myself to be technically prepared to win the match."

Kadir's belief that boxing is an art and not about winning, rather giving your best shot, transcends the ring.

He has one regret, though — the Olympic scar. The referee stopped the fight, dashing his Olympic hopes, after that nasty cut from a blow from his Cuban opponent in the second round. He cried because he knew he could have won that fight.

That's history now, like much of his life.

Kadir was born in Singapore on February 16, 1948, the youngest of Syed Abu Bakar's three children. His childhood was filled with fun and carefree abandon, growing up in a kampong in Potong Pasir. He grew up living and mixing with neighbours of all races, surrounded by nature, near five freshwater ponds, the size of two football fields.

He and his friends would horse around the ponds for hours, competing to see who could hold his breath the longest. Later in life Kadir would realise that this helped build his stamina for sports when he became the school district champion in swimming. However, he did not pursue the sport as training sessions at Yang Kit Swimming Pool, in Tanjong Pagar, was too far away from his home. When the herdsmen brought their cattle to bathe in the ponds, he rode buffaloes and cows, aping cowboys in a rodeo. How many children today or even adults can boast of riding buffaloes like Kadir did as a child? The ponds were filled with Japanese carp and, boys being boys, they would catch them and sell them to farmers who toiled in vegetable farms nearby.

He was thrilled, jumping in the air and doing somersaults. Today he sits back and admires springboard diving in international competitions, on television.

As a young boy, he played all kinds of sports except cricket. And there were particular seasons for all activities, like the windy season for kite-flying. Naturally, there was more space then to fly kites and "fight" rival kites compared to today. And when the rains came and flooded the ponds, there was abundant fish to catch without having to worry about being caught.

"Every season seems to have a reason," he said with a chuckle.

He also remembers the monsoon season when he relished playing in the rain, splashing water on friends, and wallowing in the mud. Children hardly got sick despite playing in the rain. The only thing that laid them low was chicken pox.

Unfortunately, heavy rains also caused havoc, flooding homes and forcing residents to be evacuated to St Andrew's Primary School, which stood on higher ground. And in true kampong spirit, he was there to lend a helping hand, carrying mattresses and salvaging meagre household items for others.

One day while walking past the teachers' common room in St Andrew's Primary School, he was amused to see a pair of gloves hanging in the room. Later, he learned that that the gloves were displayed to discipline students. Any boys caught fighting would be asked by the principal to put on the gloves and battle it out.

Kadir now reckons it was a deterrent, to prevent boys from fighting, as he never got to see any such bouts.

From St Andrew's Primary School, he went to Bartley Secondary School. He chose it because it was farther from home and not just a five-minute walk away like St Andrew's. He was thrilled at the prospect of riding a bus to school.

His interest in sport was derived from his father, who was the president of the Cosmos Sports Club and used to take the young lad to watch football matches at Farrer Park and Jalan Besar Stadium. The games were organised by the Singapore Amateur Football Association, (SAFA). The stadium was a wooden structure, standing close to the soccer pitch, and at times spectators would pour out to the field. Depending on which side you sat, you might get the rain or the sun. But it never really bothered you as it was all part of the fun. People rarely wore caps or carried brollies, using newspapers instead to shield themselves.

Kadir saw his first boxing match in his schooldays. In 1959, when he was 11 years old, he was given free tickets to watch Singapore boxers fight the Burmese. Inspired, he took up the sport and competed in school boxing championships.

At 18, he started training in earnest and, at 19, in 1968, he won the Singapore Open title, going on to represent the nation in the SEAP Games the following year.

Like most sporting enthusiasts of his era, he used to attend night classes after training during the day. He appreciates that his employer gave him time off to train. But he would not take it for granted and he would make up for it by going to work on weekends.

He trained at the Community Centre (CC) in Maude Road and later at Tanjong Pagar CC. According to Kadir, one of the reasons for the popularity of boxing during the 1960s and 70s was that many of the organising secretaries who managed CCs took it upon themselves to arrange and promote boxing matches. In addition, many clubs — and especially uniformed organisations like the army, navy and police — held in-house competitions.

It is common knowledge that many sportsmen believe their performance is affected by the things they do or wear. Kadir is no exception. Before a big event, he would never turn back, even if someone called him. It would be taboo. He would acknowledge them with a hand wave and proceed, but he would not turn back.

His other good-luck charm was his training outfit, which he would not wash for one or two days before a competition. It would be washed only after the event. Kadir has vivid memories of the soccer field at Farrer Park, which was once a racehorse track. Consequently, there were no special sports facilities apart from the makeshift changing rooms located where the stables once stood. The grandstand area was pulled down to accommodate Sports House, which housed the Singapore Sports Promotion Board, which was later merged into the Singapore Sports Council.

But the memory he treasures most of Farrer Park is very close to his heart. For it was where he met and fell in love with his wife.

They met after his famous victory. He won the light flyweight boxing gold medal at the 1971 SEAP Games in Kuala Lumpur, beating Vanlai Dawla of Burma, who was said to be the best boxer in Asia. The news made headlines and made him a household name.

He was then working in an accounting firm in the Chinese Chamber of Commerce, which sent him on an auditing assignment to Sports House. He reckons he was selected for the task because of his sports background.

Zalia Jaffar was working as a receptionist at Sports House. They met — and now have two grown children. Syed, the boxer, was born on February 9, 1975, one year after their marriage in 1974. Sharifah Ummu Hanni, their daughter, was born on December 22, 1979.

Zalia continues to work with the Singapore Sports Council. She has not only gained recognition as the "face and voice of SSC", but is known for her exceptional ability in recognising voices. Her work earned her a commendation from the late President Wee Kim Wee.

Kadir has come full circle, as his present training camp-cum-office for the national team is located in Farrer Park. He believes boxing is not only for men; women can excel, too, as some are showing their skills in Muay Thai and other combat sports. For sports to flourish, he feels, there has to be commitment and support — commitment from the athletes and support from various organisations and the government. To overcome our small size and population, we have to work doubly hard, he adds, citing Suriname, which has produced an Olympic champion, the swimmer Anthony Nesty, who won the gold in the 100-metre butterfly in 1988. Sports schools are also needed for those who are not academically inclined, said Kadir.

Fishing was and is still his hobby. However, he no longer fishes in ponds, but ventures to neighbouring Malaysia and Indonesia to fish in the open seas, with his childhood friends who banter about their unforgettable childhood memories. Fishing teaches patience, which is also needed in sports, says the former boxing champion, who should know. You can't lose your head: you have to bide your time, wait for the opportunity to strike.

Singapore's one and only boxing Olympian is not resting on his laurels. Keen to promote boxing, he offers training at the Kadir Boxing School in Guillemard Road for only a nominal sum of $40 a month for five weekly sessions. He said he actually subsidised the cost.

He also gives talks in schools to promote the sport. The former champion, who once sparred for medals, now hunts for talent. Most may prefer the ringside to the ring. The man himself bears a scar from a cut above the eye. But, to hear him speak, boxing is a performing art where you go toe to toe, not dance cheek to cheek, with your opposite number.

BY ABHIJIT NAG

RUNNER-PHILOSOPHER

Singapore's fastest man UK Shyam's life before and after the record he set in 10 seconds.

He chased his dream in running gear and became Singapore's fastest man. He took only 10 seconds to streak into the record books, but only after years of struggle. Lean and tall, a good-looking hunk who looks much younger than his 39 years, Umaglia Kancanangai Shyam Dhuleep, popularly known as UK Shyam, has looked at life from both sides now. He has been down and out and scaled the heights of success.

The national record he set with a 100-metre dash in 10.37 seconds at the World University Games in Beijing in 2001 is still unbroken. He repeated that feat with another 100-metre dash in 10.37 seconds again, winning the silver medal at the 21st South East Asian (SEA) Games in Kuala Lumpur later that year. No Singaporean has run that distance that fast yet.

Meanwhile, he has found his feet in academe. The athlete who once waited at tables is a lecturer now at Hwa Chong Institution, teaching philosophy and political science. Besides holding forth on Sartre and Foucault, his favourite philosophers, he could give his students lessons in perseverance and dedication. Speaking from experience, he would presumably slip in a word of advice: Don't neglect your studies, whatever you do. GPA counts.

"I got this job because of my GPA," he said. After a day in class, he was geared for the track, wearing a baseball cap, sleeveless tees and knee-length tights, a rucksack on his shoulder. He has married his girlfriend, Hui Ping, who also teaches at Nanyang Girls High school, and settled down. But, "once a runner, always a runner," said the four-times SEA Games medallist, who still hits the Kallang practice track three times a week.

Grabbing a quick bite at the Kent Ridge cafeteria, the boyish-looking lecturer didn't look like he could hurt a fly, but he had his run-ins with sports officials when he was running for

Singapore. As a National University of Singapore (NUS) arts undergraduate, he occasionally skipped training and meets to the chagrin of the bosses. But he had to study for his exams. And that's what's putting food on his table now — his GPA.

NUS was not his first choice. He wanted to study abroad so he could compete with the best and improve as an athlete. He got admission to an Australian university (UNSW) in the year 2000, expecting to be funded by the athletic association. But, two days before his flight, he was informed that the money would not be forthcoming for overseas studies. It was a triple blow. He could not pay his way through college abroad. There was no place in the local university. And he had blown a hole in the bank account, having paid for university admission and the air ticket himself (finished all his savings which was given by his dad). He would eventually get back the money from the university. But, meanwhile, he had to support himself, his divorced mother and his younger sister.

He worked at a restaurant to make ends meet. Moved by his plight, champion swimmer Ang Peng Siong offered him a part-time job at his swim school and encouraged him to keep on training. Shyam also persuaded Chilean coach Pedro Acuna to train him. The hard work paid off. Shyam won the 2001 Hong Kong Open in 10.45 seconds, qualifying for the SEA Games. Before the SEA Games, he also set a new national record at the world university games.

Shyam smiled at the memory of August 27, 2001, a bright summer's day in Beijing. The others watched amused as the Singaporeans suddenly whooped and jumped with joy. It was only a routine run during the heats. But the Singaporeans had reason to celebrate. A record had been broken that had stood for 38 years, set by the legendary C Kunalan. Kunalan had run the 100 metres in 10.38 seconds to qualify for the semi-finals in the 1968 Mexico Olympics. Now, nearly four decades later, a 25-year-old had shaved 0.01 second off that record and made history.

"On the day he broke the record, his phone never stopped ringing", recalled his sister, Sangeetha. "Many of his fans and well-wishers called to congratulate him. One of his fans even sent a huge bouquet of roses, studded with chocolates."

Shyam was the first athlete to be placed on Singapore Sports Council's inaugural Athlete Career Training (ACT) Programme in 2001. He was also awarded the Singapore National Olympic Council's Meritorious Award that year.

His mum knew her boy could run from the time he was nine years old, in Primary 4. She went to cheer him on Sports Day at Parry Primary School and saw him win all the four events in which he took part. "My spirits were lifted when I saw him run and later when his name was called four times. I realised that he had a distinct interest in athletics," said Madam Sujatha Fernando.

Born on July 1, 1976, "Shyam was the most cherubic-looking baby born into our family circle," recalled his aunt, Lalitha Perera, his mother's sister, whom he fondly calls Amma ("mother" in Sinhala). "He had brown curls clinging to his forehead, a golden wheat complexion and big eyes. He had some breathing difficulties at birth. We were only allowed to peep at him through the glass pane. My husband named him Shyam Dhuleep. He became the darling of our family," she added.

He loved to run and hated coming second best, recalled his aunt. "My elder twin daughter Yasodha remembers Shyam's competitive nature. She was in lower secondary and he in primary school. The two of them raced along the little road where my parents' house stood. He was never too happy when his cousin won, but he never wanted a handicap," she added.

When he was 12, his mother remembers him tirelessly running the hilly terrain outside their home in Teo Hock Road. He would challenge his sister, Sangeeta, to run as fast as she could to fetch a glass of water to rejuvenate his leg muscles. Running like that, she too became an outstanding school athlete.

Shyam attended St Andrew's Secondary School and joined the rugby team. He enjoyed sport, but gave it up because his mum felt it was too rough, as he used to come home bruised. He still has a passion for rugby. Every Saturday, he trains the Singapore rugby sevens for the upcoming SEA Games, helping them gain speed and power.

He also played soccer in school. Impressed by his speed as he ran with the ball, his teacher, Thomas Tan, suggested he switch to athletics when he was 16.

That was the beginning of his glorious run. Shyam, who went on to attend Raffles Junior College and complete his national service, picked up his first SEA Games medal in 1997. He was the anchor-man in the Singapore relay team, which won the bronze at the Jakarta SEA Games.

For several years starting from 1999, he wanted to compete in the 100 metres, but sports officials insisted he focus on the relay, discounting his chances in the individual event till he proved them wrong by winning the Hong Kong Open and breaking Kunalan's record in 2001.

In the end, Shyam took part in the 22nd SEA Games in Hanoi in December 2003 and helped Singapore win the silver in the 4x100 metres relay. He also helped Singapore to a bronze in the same event in the 2005 SEA Games in Manila.

He won four SEA Games medals, one at every Games from 1997 to 2005. But he gave the silver medal he won in Hanoi to Yusof Alias, the reserve runner. "I felt bad for Yusof because he should have been in the final squad," he said. TODAY reported it under the headline, "A kind gesture".

Photo courtesy of Colin Wee

As a student and teacher of philosophy, Shyam's interests range from religion to modern thinkers. As an athlete, his favourite runner is Linford Christie.

"He is very idealistic, with a strong mind. Like most teenagers, Shyam disliked having to toe the line. His rebellious, independent nature stood him in very good stead, moulding a platform for his passionate desire to succeed," said his aunt, Lalitha, who knows him well.

"He stayed with me and my family when he was in Sec 1 and 2 at St Andrew's," she adds. "I used to drop him off before I went to a school nearby where I held an administrative post. She cannot forget his athletic feats. "I have beautiful memories of Shyam's success at the SEA Games in KL in September 2001," she said. "I travelled by coach with his mother. His 100-metre dash was witnessed by his parents and many well-wishers. The thunderous applause deafened our ears as Shyam draped himself with the Singapore flag as he broke Kunalan's record as the fastest man of Singapore but lost the gold by a whisker. We were all delirious with excitement."

Shyam's father, Cyril, came all the way from Manila to see him run at the Kuala Lumpur SEA Games. Delighted, Shyam hugged his parents, who sat together, before receiving his medal. Shyam is grateful to Olympics swimmer Ang Peng Siong and coach Pedro Acuna for helping him achieve his dream. Ang not only gave him a job, but bought him vitamins and health supplements and helped him apply to American universities. Recalling the encouragement he received from Ang, he says people achieve greater heights when they are motivated rather than dictated to.

Shyam did a double degree in philosophy and political science at NUS and then got a postgraduate diploma in education at the National Institute of Education in Nanyang

Technological University. He taught at Nanyang Girls' High School before joining Hwa Chong. He took up teaching, he said, because he wanted to "give back" to the community. He was also influenced by his cousin, Sanjay Perera, son of the late broadcaster Ananda Perera, with whom he lived in his teens. It was his cousin who inspired him to read various writers and philosophers. Now it's his turn to share his knowledge and appreciation with his students. In his book, however, there's more to life than books. The junior college lecturer, who still runs for recreation, stressed the importance of sports. The lessons learnt in sports can't be had in the classroom, he said. He should know, having been both athlete and academic — Singapore's once and still fastest man.